Of Our Spiritual Strivings

Afterall Books

Christina Quarles / W.E.B. Du Bois

Two Works

OF OUR SPIRITUAL STRIVINGS
W.E.B. DU BOIS

This edition of 'Of Our Spiritual Strivings' reproduces the text in the first edition of *The Souls of Black Folk*, published by A.C. McClurg and Company in April 1903. The essay is a revision of 'Strivings of the Negro People', published in *Atlantic Monthly* in August 1897.

O water, voice of my heart, crying in the sand,
　All night long crying with a mournful cry,
As I lie and listen, and cannot understand
　　The voice of my heart in my side or the voice of the sea,
　O water, crying for rest, is it I, is it I?
　　All night long the water is crying to me.

Unresting water, there shall never be rest
　Till the last moon droop and the last tide fail,
And the fire of the end begin to burn in the west;
　　And the heart shall be weary and wonder and cry like
　　the sea,
　All life long crying without avail,
　　As the water all night long is crying to me.

–Arthur Symons

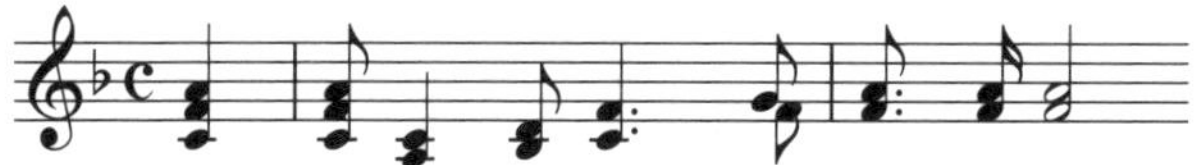

Between me and the other world there is ever an unasked question: unasked by some through feelings of delicacy; by others through the difficulty of rightly framing it. All, nevertheless, flutter round it. They approach me in a half-hesitant sort of way, eye me curiously or compassionately, and then, instead of saying directly, How does it feel to be a problem? they say, I know an excellent colored man in my town; or, I fought at Mechanicsville; or, Do not these Southern outrages make your blood boil? At these I smile, or am interested, or reduce the boiling to a simmer, as the occasion may require. To the real question, How does it feel to be a problem? I answer seldom a word.

And yet, being a problem is a strange experience, – peculiar even for one who has never been anything else, save perhaps in babyhood and in Europe. It is in the early days of rollicking boyhood that the revelation first bursts upon one, all in a day, as it were. I remember well when the shadow swept across me. I was a little thing, away up in the hills of New England, where the dark Housatonic winds between Hoosac and Taghkanic to the sea. In a wee wooden schoolhouse, something put it into the boys' and girls' heads to buy gorgeous visiting-cards – ten cents a package – and exchange. The exchange was merry, till one girl, a tall newcomer, refused my card, – refused it peremptorily, with a glance. Then it dawned upon me with a certain suddenness that I was different from the others; or like, mayhap, in heart and life and longing, but shut out from their world by a vast veil. I had thereafter no desire to tear down that veil, to creep through; I held all beyond it in common contempt, and lived above it in a region of blue sky and great wandering shadows. That sky was bluest when I could beat my mates at examination time, or beat them at a foot-race, or even beat their stringy heads. Alas, with the years all this fine contempt began to fade; for the worlds I longed for, and all their dazzling opportunities, were theirs, not mine. But they should not keep these prizes, I said; some, all, I would wrest from them. Just how I would do it I could never decide: by reading law, by healing the sick, by telling the wonderful tales that swam in my head, – some way. With other black boys the strife was not so fiercely sunny: their youth shrunk into tasteless sycophancy, or into silent hatred of the pale world about them and mocking distrust of everything white; or wasted itself in a bitter cry, Why did God make me an outcast and a stranger in mine own house? The shades of the prison-house closed round about us all: walls strait and stubborn to the whitest, but relentlessly narrow, tall, and unscalable to sons of night who must plod darkly on in resignation, or beat unavailing palms against the stone, or steadily, half hopelessly, watch the streak of blue above.

After the Egyptian and Indian, the Greek and Roman, the Teuton and Mongolian, the Negro is a sort of seventh son, born with a veil, and gifted with second-sight in this American world, – a world which yields him no true self-consciousness, but only lets him see himself through the revelation of the other world. It is a peculiar sensation, this double-consciousness, this sense of always looking at one's self through the eyes of others, of measuring one's soul by the tape of a world that looks on in amused contempt and pity. One ever feels his two-ness, – an American, a Negro; two souls, two thoughts, two unreconciled strivings; two warring ideals in one dark body, whose dogged strength alone keeps it from being torn asunder.

The history of the American Negro is the history of this strife,
– this longing to attain self-conscious manhood, to merge his
double self into a better and truer self. In this merging he wishes
neither of the older selves to be lost. He would not Africanize
America, for America has too much to teach the world and
Africa. He would not bleach his Negro soul in a flood of white
Americanism, for he knows that Negro blood has a message for
the world. He simply wishes to make it possible for a man to be
both a Negro and an American, without being cursed and spit
upon by his fellows, without having the doors of Opportunity
closed roughly in his face.

This, then, is the end of his striving: to be a co-worker in the
kingdom of culture, to escape both death and isolation, to
husband and use his best powers and his latent genius. These
powers of body and mind have in the past been strangely
wasted, dispersed, or forgotten. The shadow of a mighty Negro
past flits through the tale of Ethiopia the Shadowy and of Egypt
the Sphinx. Throughout history, the powers of single black
men flash here and there like falling stars, and die sometimes
before the world has rightly gauged their brightness. Here in
America, in the few days since Emancipation, the black man's
turning hither and thither in hesitant and doubtful striving has
often made his very strength to lose effectiveness, to seem like
absence of power, like weakness. And yet it is not weakness,
– it is the contradiction of double aims. The double-aimed
struggle of the black artisan – on the one hand to escape white
contempt for a nation of mere hewers of wood and drawers
of water, and on the other hand to plough and nail and dig for
a poverty-stricken horde – could only result in making him a
poor craftsman, for he had but half a heart in either cause. By
the poverty and ignorance of his people, the Negro minister
or doctor was tempted toward quackery and demagogy; and
by the criticism of the other world, toward ideals that made
him ashamed of his lowly tasks. The would-be black savant
was confronted by the paradox that the knowledge his people
needed was a twice told tale to his white neighbors, while the
knowledge which would teach the white world was Greek to his
own flesh and blood. The innate love of harmony and beauty
that set the ruder souls of his people a-dancing and a-singing
raised but confusion and doubt in the soul of the black artist;

for the beauty revealed to him was the soul-beauty of a race which his larger audience despised, and he could not articulate the message of another people. This waste of double aims, this seeking to satisfy two unreconciled ideals, has wrought sad havoc with the courage and faith and deeds of ten thousand thousand people, – has sent them often wooing false gods and invoking false means of salvation, and at times has even seemed about to make them ashamed of themselves.

Away back in the days of bondage they thought to see in one divine event the end of all doubt and disappointment; few men ever worshipped Freedom with half such unquestioning faith as did the American Negro for two centuries. To him, so far as he thought and dreamed, slavery was indeed the sum of all villainies, the cause of all sorrow, the root of all prejudice; Emancipation was the key to a promised land of sweeter beauty than ever stretched before the eyes of wearied Israelites. In song and exhortation swelled one refrain – Liberty; in his tears and curses the God he implored had Freedom in his right hand. At last it came, – suddenly, fearfully, like a dream. With one wild carnival of blood and passion came the message in his own plaintive cadences: –

> 'Shout, O children!
> Shout, you're free!
> For God has bought your liberty!'

Years have passed away since then, – ten, twenty, forty; forty years of national life, forty years of renewal and development, and yet the swarthy spectre sits in its accustomed seat at the Nation's feast. In vain do we cry to this our vastest social problem: –

> 'Take any shape but that, and my firm nerves
> Shall never tremble!'

The Nation has not yet found peace from its sins; the freedman has not yet found in freedom his promised land. Whatever of good may have come in these years of change, the shadow of a deep disappointment rests upon the Negro people, – a disappointment all the more bitter because the unattained ideal was unbounded save by the simple ignorance of a lowly people.

The first decade was merely a prolongation of the vain search for freedom, the boon that seemed ever barely to elude their grasp, – like a tantalizing will-o'-the-wisp, maddening and misleading the headless host. The holocaust of war, the terrors of the Ku-Klux Klan, the lies of carpet-baggers, the disorganization of industry, and the contradictory advice of friends and foes, left the bewildered serf with no new watchword beyond the old cry for freedom. As the time flew, however, he began to grasp a new idea. The ideal of liberty demanded for its attainment powerful means, and these the Fifteenth Amendment gave him. The ballot, which before he had looked upon as a visible sign of freedom, he now regarded as the chief means of gaining and perfecting the liberty with which war had partially endowed him. And why not? Had not votes made war and emancipated millions? Had not votes enfranchised the freedmen? Was anything impossible to a power that had done all this? A million black men started with renewed zeal to vote themselves into the kingdom. So the decade flew away, the revolution of 1876 came, and left the half-free serf weary, wondering, but still inspired. Slowly but steadily, in the following years, a new vision began gradually to replace the dream of political power, – a powerful movement, the rise of another ideal to guide the unguided, another pillar of fire by night after a clouded day. It was the ideal of 'book-learning'; the curiosity, born of compulsory ignorance, to know and test the power of the cabalistic letters of the white man, the longing to know. Here at last seemed to have been discovered the mountain path to Canaan; longer than the highway of Emancipation and law, steep and rugged, but straight, leading to heights high enough to overlook life.

Up the new path the advance guard toiled, slowly, heavily, doggedly; only those who have watched and guided the faltering feet, the misty minds, the dull understandings, of the dark pupils of these schools know how faithfully, how piteously, this people strove to learn. It was weary work. The cold statistician wrote down the inches of progress here and there, noted also where here and there a foot had slipped or some one had fallen. To the tired climbers, the horizon was ever dark, the mists were often cold, the Canaan was always dim and far away. If, however, the vistas disclosed as yet no goal, no resting-place, little but flattery and criticism, the journey at least gave leisure for reflection and self-examination; it changed the child of Emancipation to the youth with dawning self-consciousness, self-realization, self respect. In those sombre forests of his striving his own soul rose before him, and he saw himself, – darkly as through a veil; and yet he saw in himself some faint revelation of his power, of his mission. He began to have a dim feeling that, to attain his place in the world, he must be himself, and not another. For the first time he sought to analyze the burden he bore upon his back, that dead-weight of social degradation partially masked behind a half-named Negro problem. He felt his poverty; without a cent, without a home, without land, tools, or savings, he had entered into competition with rich, landed, skilled neighbors. To be a poor man is hard, but to be a poor race in a land of dollars is the very bottom of hardships. He felt the weight of his ignorance, –not simply of letters, but of life, of business, of the humanities; the accumulated sloth and shirking and awkwardness of decades and centuries shackled his hands and feet. Nor was his burden all poverty and ignorance. The red stain of bastardy, which two centuries of systematic legal defilement of Negro women had stamped upon his race, meant not only the loss of ancient African chastity, but also the hereditary weight of a mass of corruption from white adulterers, threatening almost the obliteration of the Negro home.

A people thus handicapped ought not to be asked to race with the world, but rather allowed to give all its time and thought to its own social problems. But alas! while sociologists gleefully count his bastards and his prostitutes, the very soul of the toiling, sweating black man is darkened by the shadow of a vast despair. Men call the shadow prejudice, and learnedly explain it as the natural defence of culture against barbarism, learning against ignorance, purity against crime, the 'higher' against the 'lower' races. To which the Negro cries Amen! and swears that to so much of this strange prejudice as is founded on just homage to civilization, culture, righteousness, and progress, he humbly bows and meekly does obeisance. But before that nameless prejudice that leaps beyond all this he stands helpless, dismayed, and well-nigh speechless; before that personal disrespect and mockery, the ridicule and systematic humiliation, the distortion of fact and wanton license of fancy, the cynical ignoring of the better and the boisterous welcoming of the worse, the all-pervading desire to inculcate disdain for everything black, from Toussaint to the devil, – before this there rises a sickening despair that would disarm and discourage any nation save that black host to whom 'discouragement' is an unwritten word.

But the facing of so vast a prejudice could not but bring the inevitable self-questioning, self-disparagement, and lowering of ideals which ever accompany repression and breed in an atmosphere of contempt and hate. Whisperings and portents came borne upon the four winds: Lo! we are diseased and dying, cried the dark hosts; we cannot write, our voting is vain; what need of education, since we must always cook and serve? And the Nation echoed and enforced this self-criticism, saying: Be content to be servants, and nothing more; what need of higher culture for half-men? Away with the black man's ballot, by force or fraud, – and behold the suicide of a race! Nevertheless, out of the evil came something of good, – the more careful adjustment of education to real life, the clearer perception of the Negroes' social responsibilities, and the sobering realization of the meaning of progress.

So dawned the time of *Sturm und Drang*: storm and stress today rocks our little boat on the mad waters of the world-sea; there is within and without the sound of conflict, the burning of body and rending of soul; inspiration strives with doubt, and faith with vain questionings. The bright ideals of the past, – physical freedom, political power, the training of brains and the training of hands, – all these in turn have waxed and waned, until even the last grows dim and overcast. Are they all wrong, – all false? No, not that, but each alone was over-simple and incomplete, –the dreams of a credulous race-childhood, or the fond imaginings of the other world which does not know and does not want to know our power. To be really true, all these ideals must be melted and welded into one. The training of the schools we need to-day more than ever, – the training of deft hands, quick eyes and ears, and above all the broader, deeper, higher culture of gifted minds and pure hearts. The power of the ballot we need in sheer self-defence, – else what shall save us from a second slavery? Freedom, too, the long-sought, we still seek, – the freedom of life and limb, the freedom to work and think, the freedom to love and aspire. Work, culture, liberty, – all these we need, not singly but together, not successively but together, each growing and aiding each, and all striving toward that vaster ideal that swims before the Negro people, the ideal of human brotherhood, gained through the unifying ideal of Race; the ideal of fostering and developing the traits and talents of the Negro, not in opposition to or contempt for other races, but rather in large conformity to the greater ideals of the American Republic, in order that some day on American soil two world-races may give each to each those characteristics both so sadly lack. We the darker ones come even now not altogether empty-handed: there are to-day no truer exponents of the pure human spirit of the Declaration of Independence than the American Negroes; there is no true American music but the wild sweet melodies of the Negro slave; the American fairy tales and folklore are Indian and African; and, all in all, we black men seem the sole oasis of simple faith and reverence in a dusty desert of dollars and smartness. Will America be poorer if she replace her brutal dyspeptic blundering with light-hearted but determined Negro humility? or her coarse and cruel wit with loving jovial good-humor? or her vulgar music with the soul of the Sorrow Songs?

Merely a concrete test of the underlying principles of the great republic is the Negro Problem, and the spiritual striving of the freedmen's sons is the travail of souls whose burden is almost beyond the measure of their strength, but who bear it in the name of an historic race, in the name of this the land of their fathers' fathers, and in the name of human opportunity.

CHRISTINA QUARLES

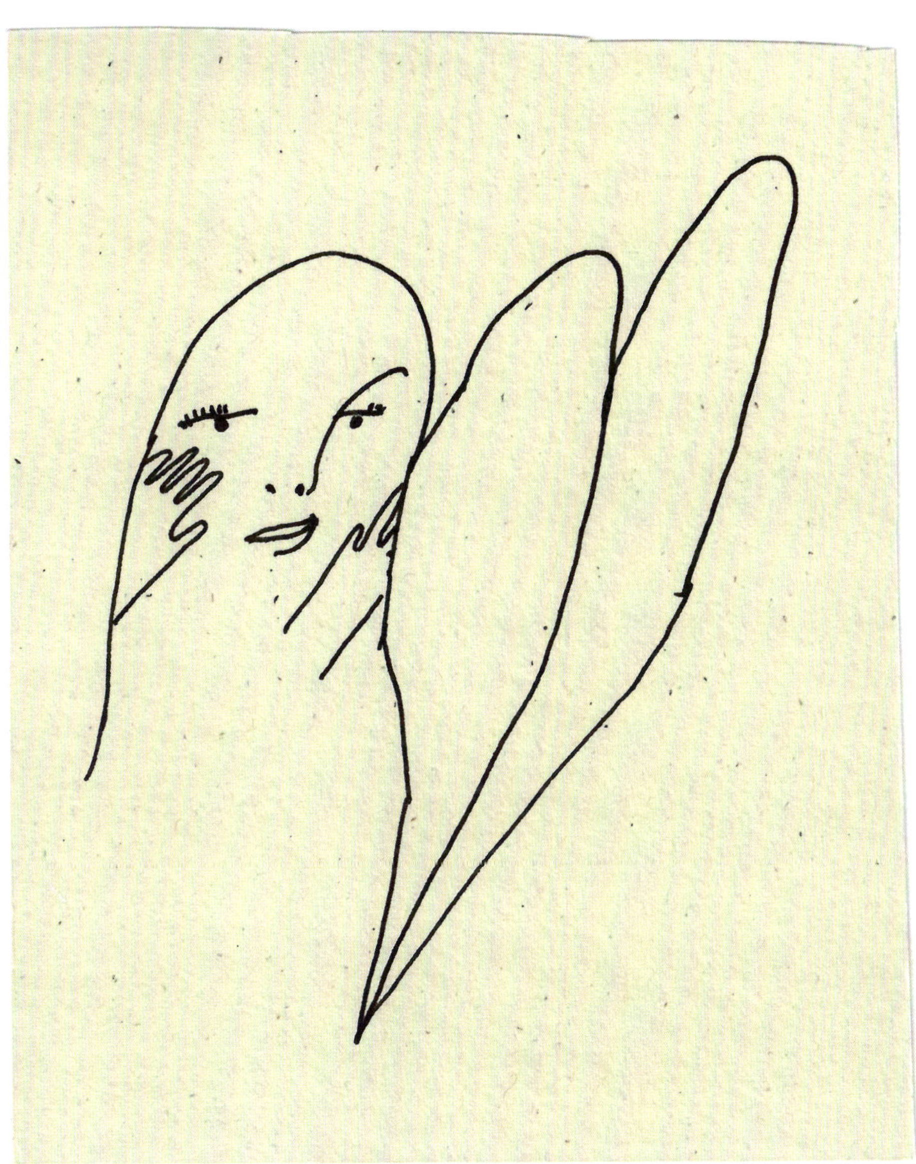

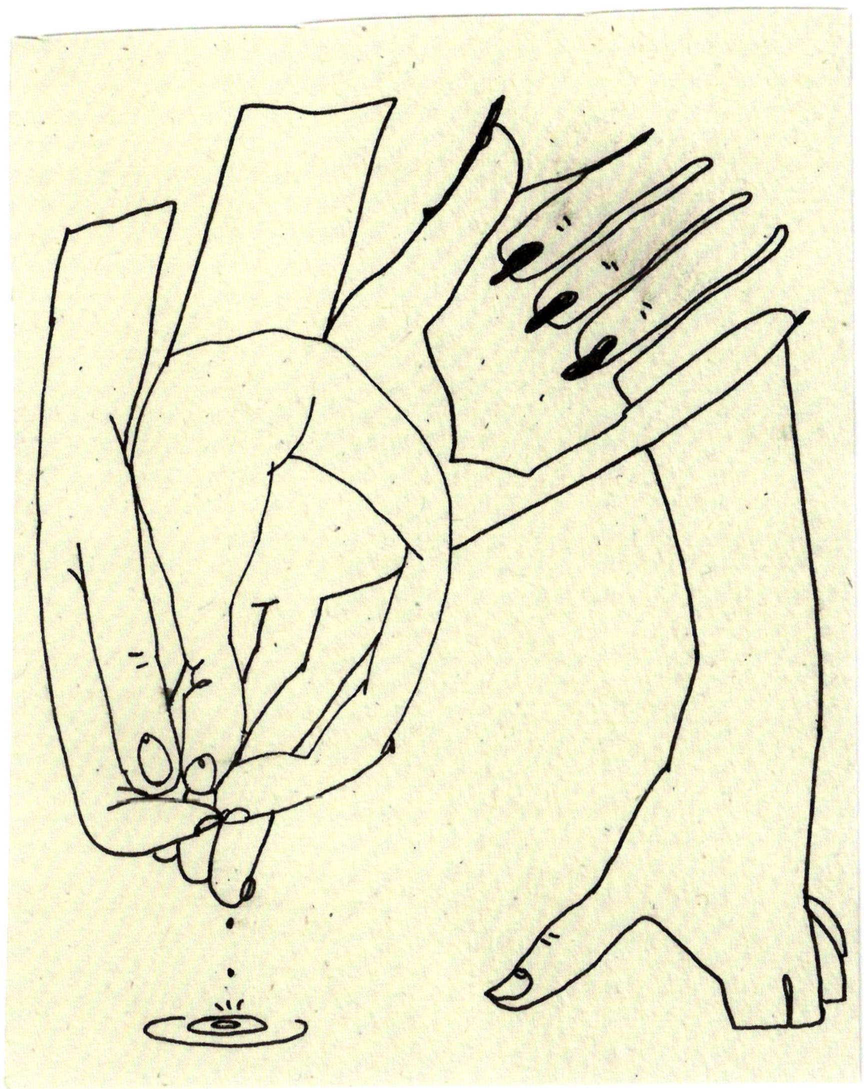

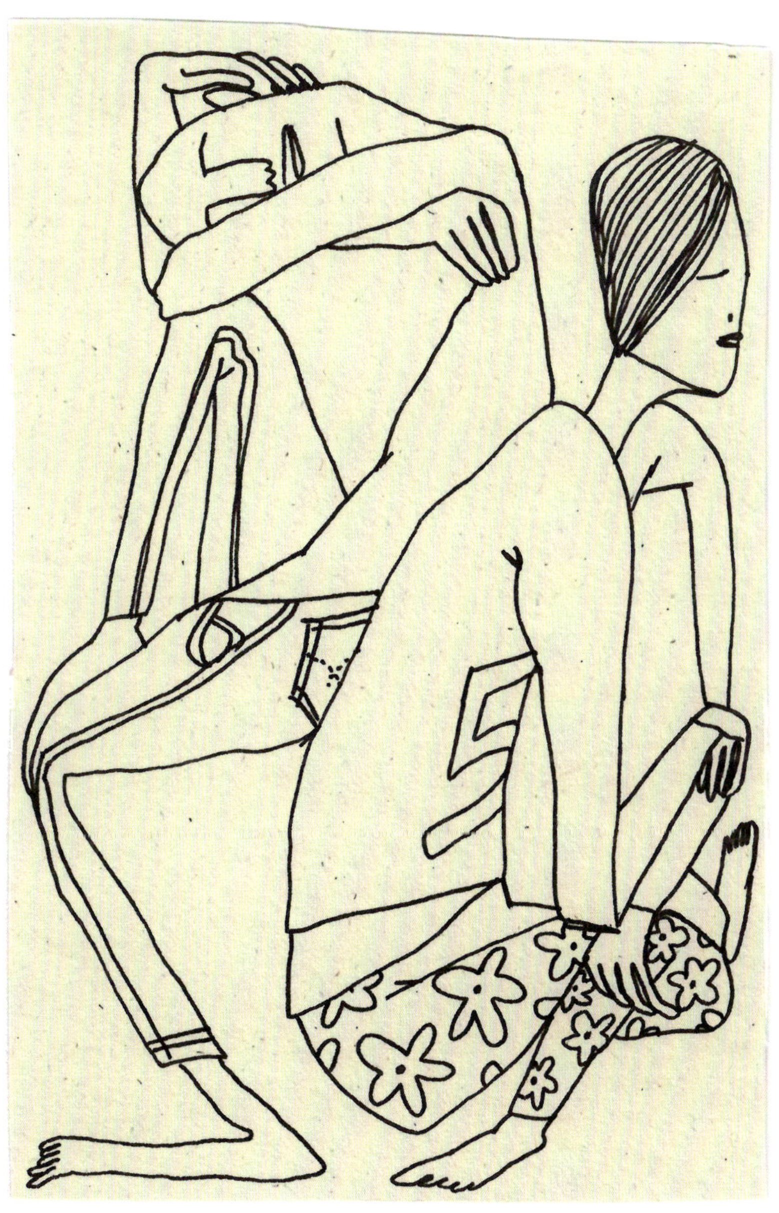

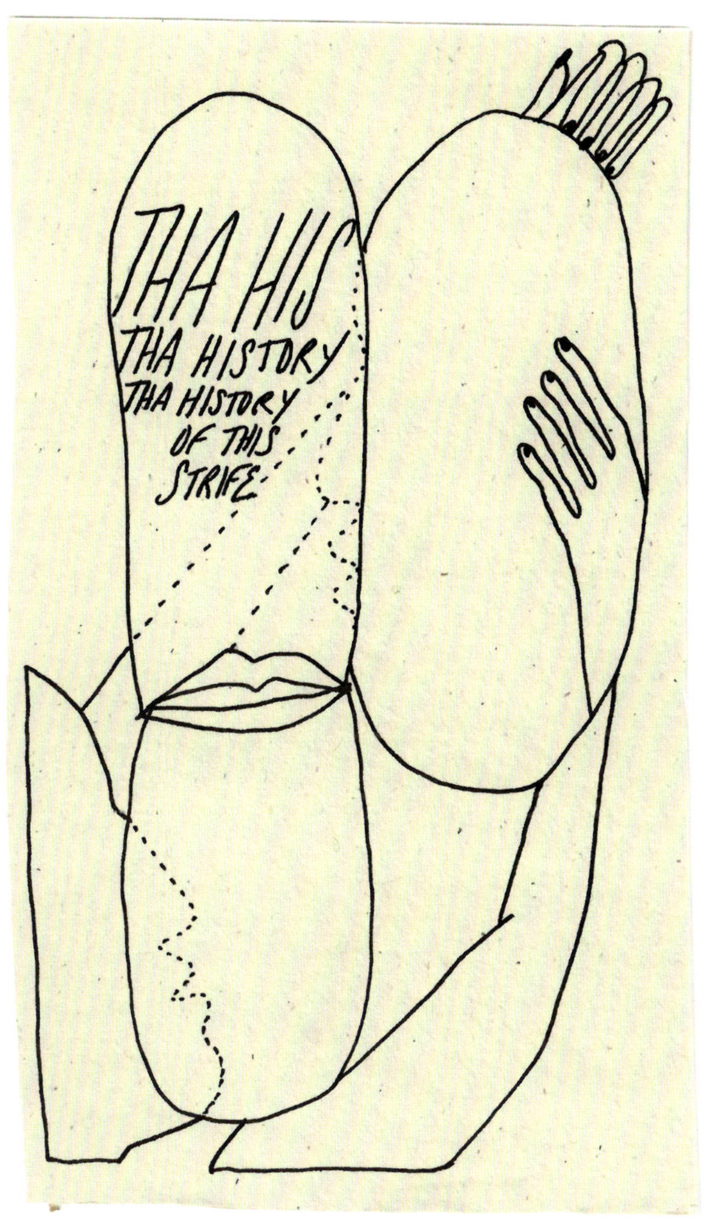

THA HIS
THA HISTORY
THA HISTORY
OF THIS
STRIFE

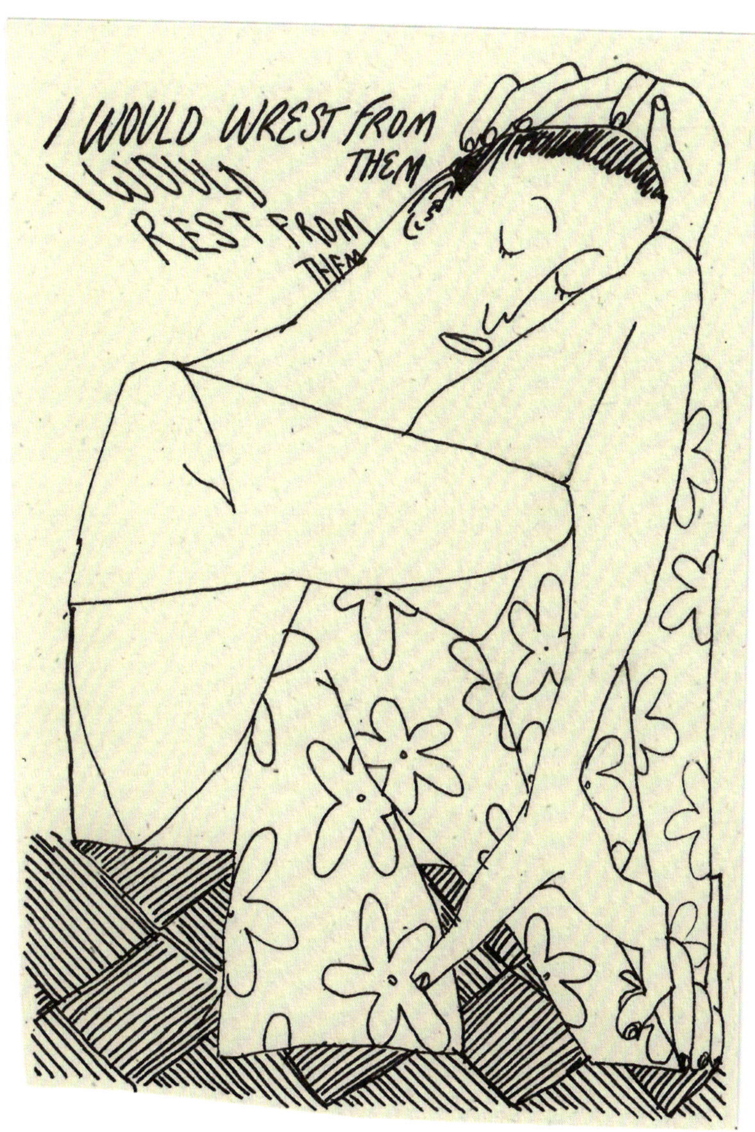

I WOULD WREST FROM THEM
I WOULD REST FROM THEM

IN THIS, THA LAND OF
MY FATHERS'
FATHERS

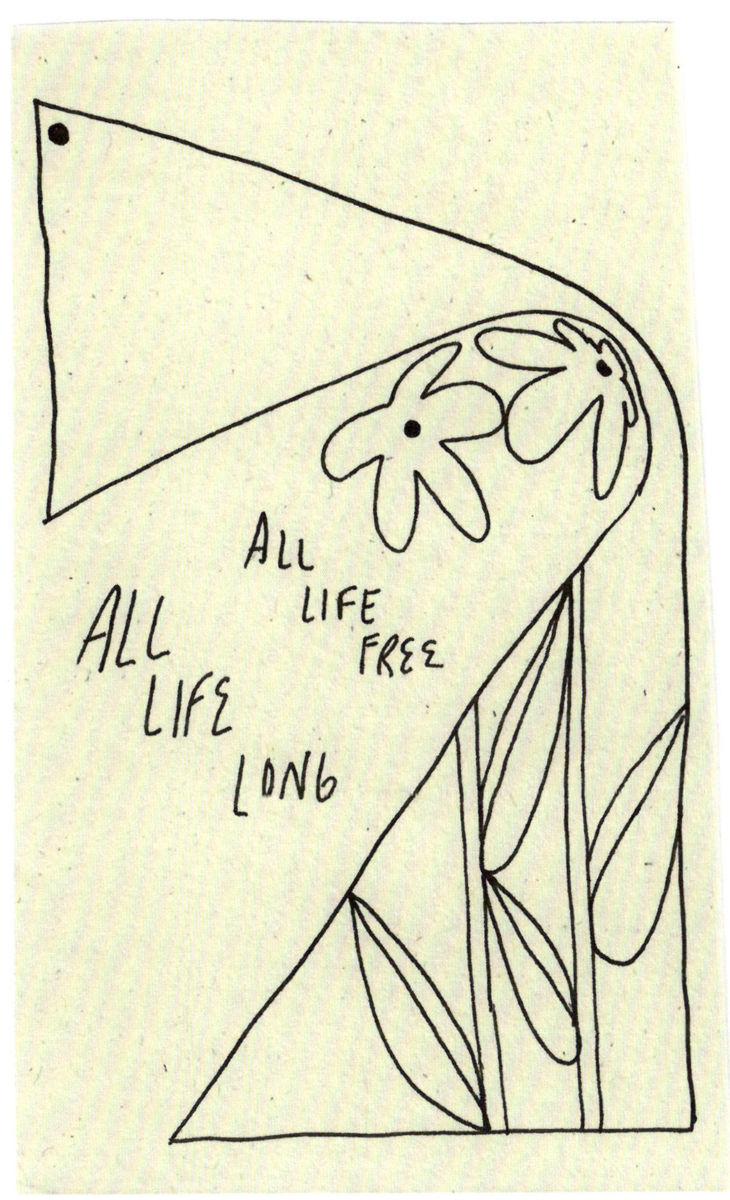

ALL
LIFE
FREE

ALL
LIFE
LONG

TAKE ANY SHAPE
(BUT THAT)

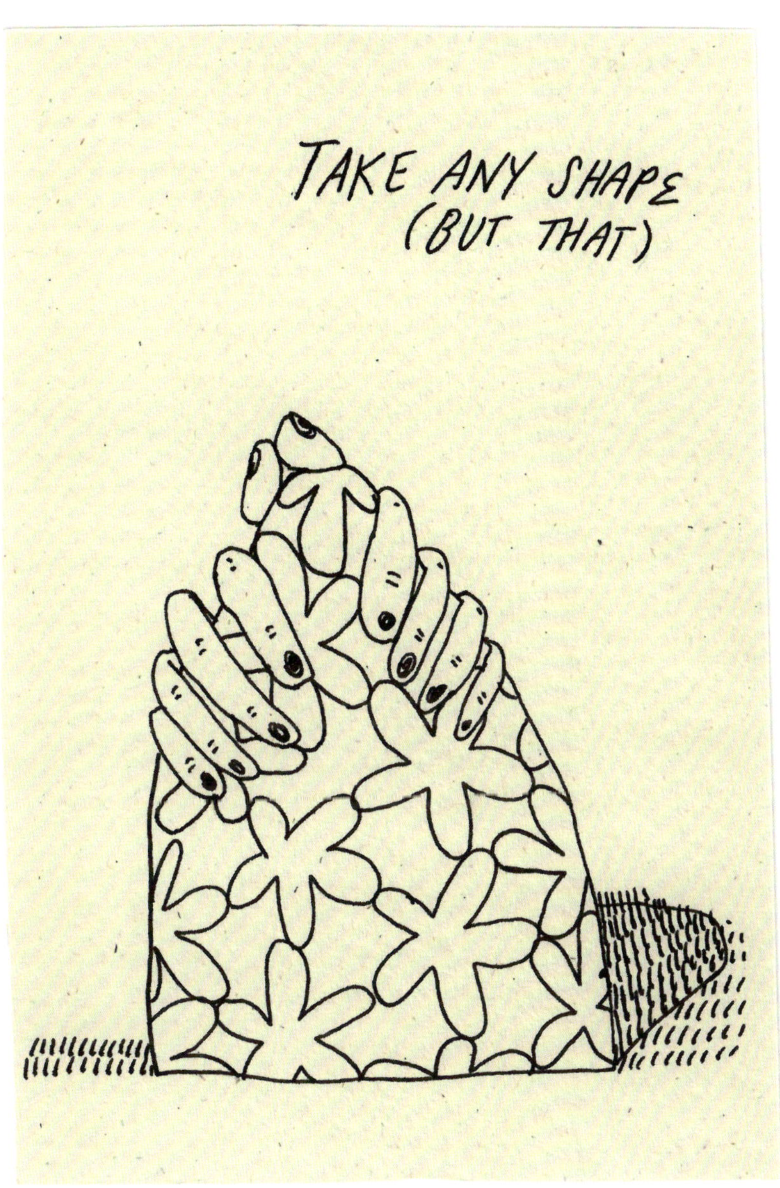

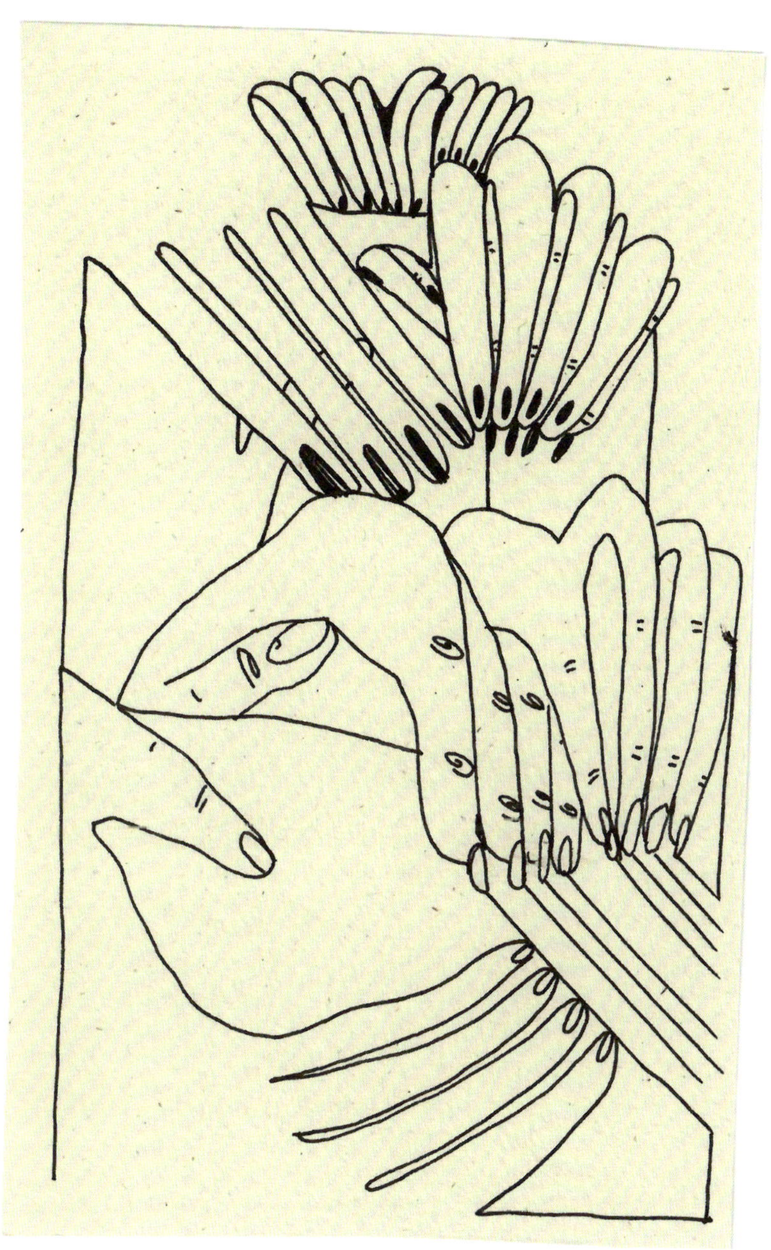

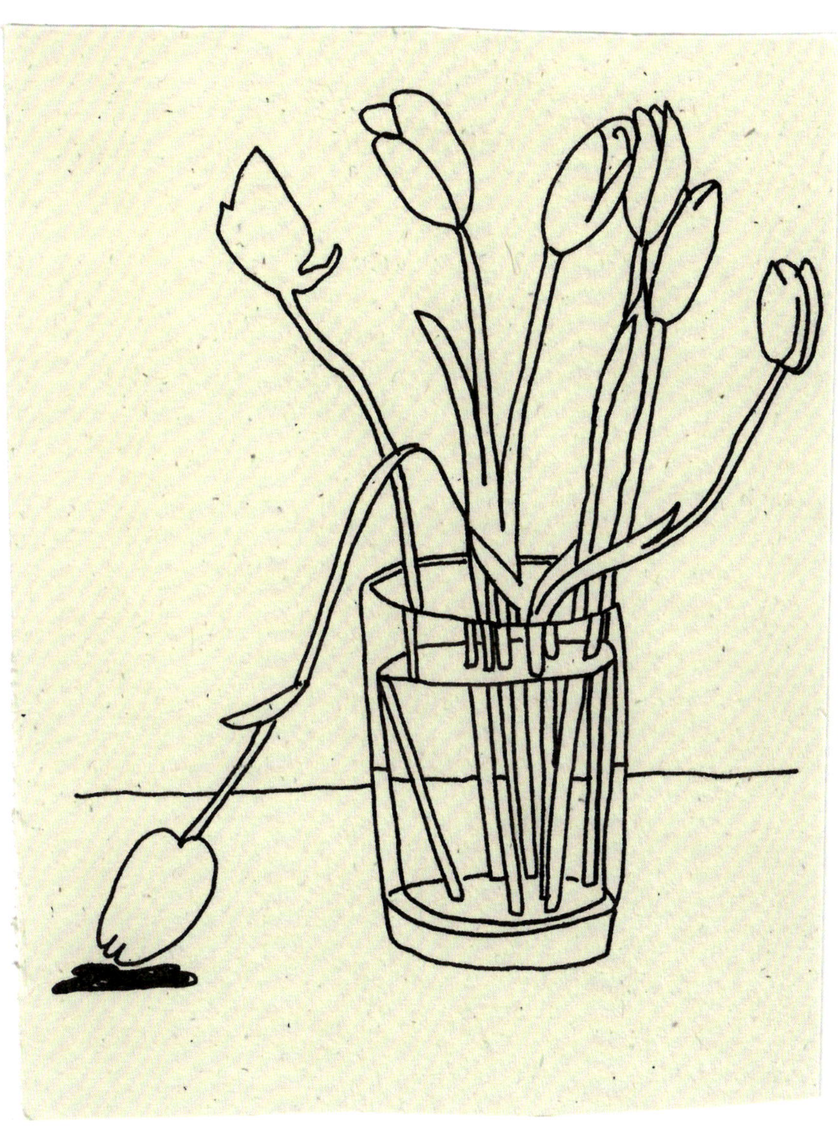

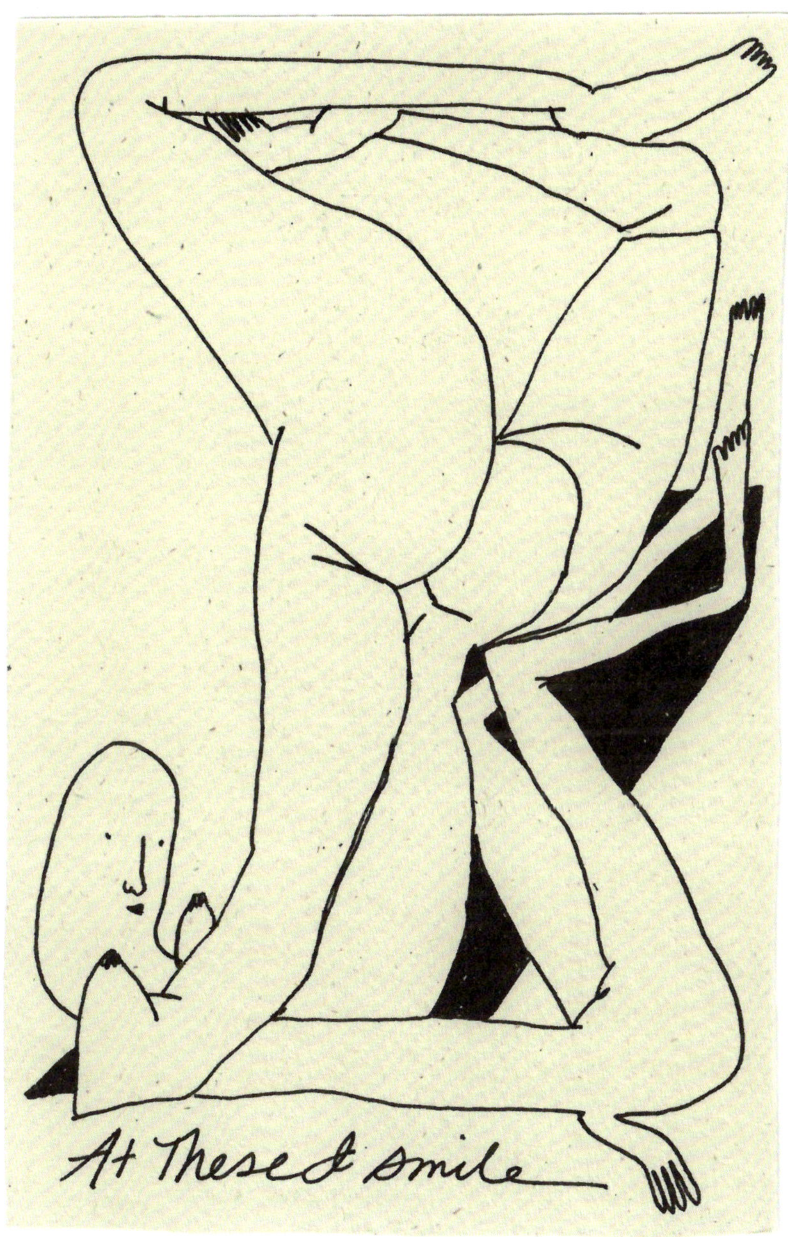
At These I Smile

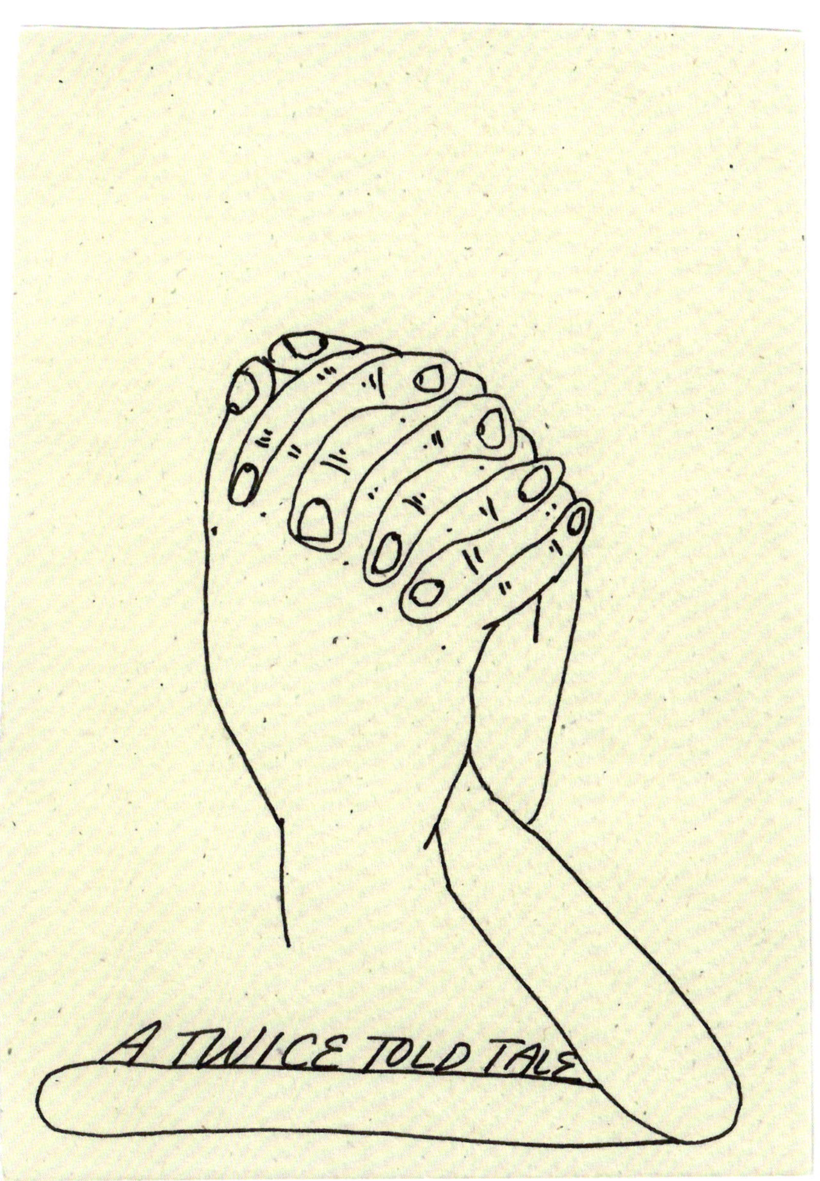
A TWICE TOLD TALE

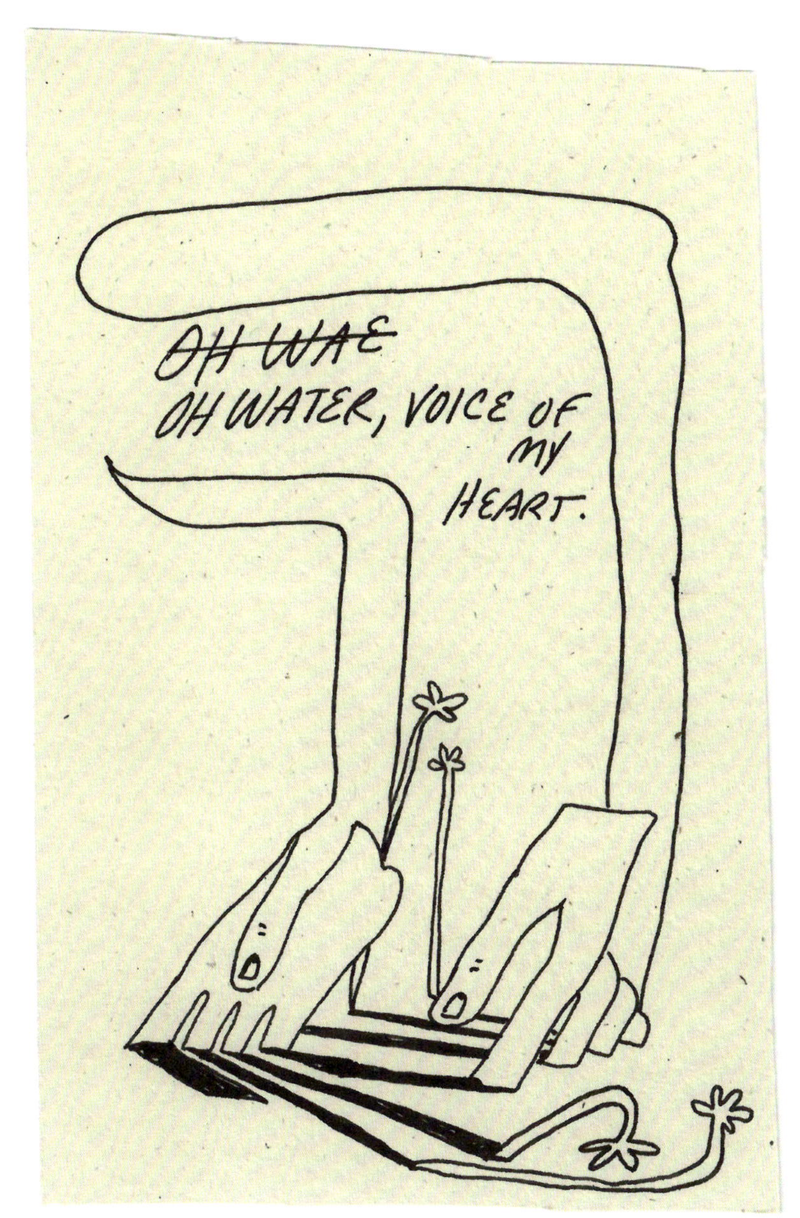

OH WAE
OH WATER, VOICE OF MY HEART.

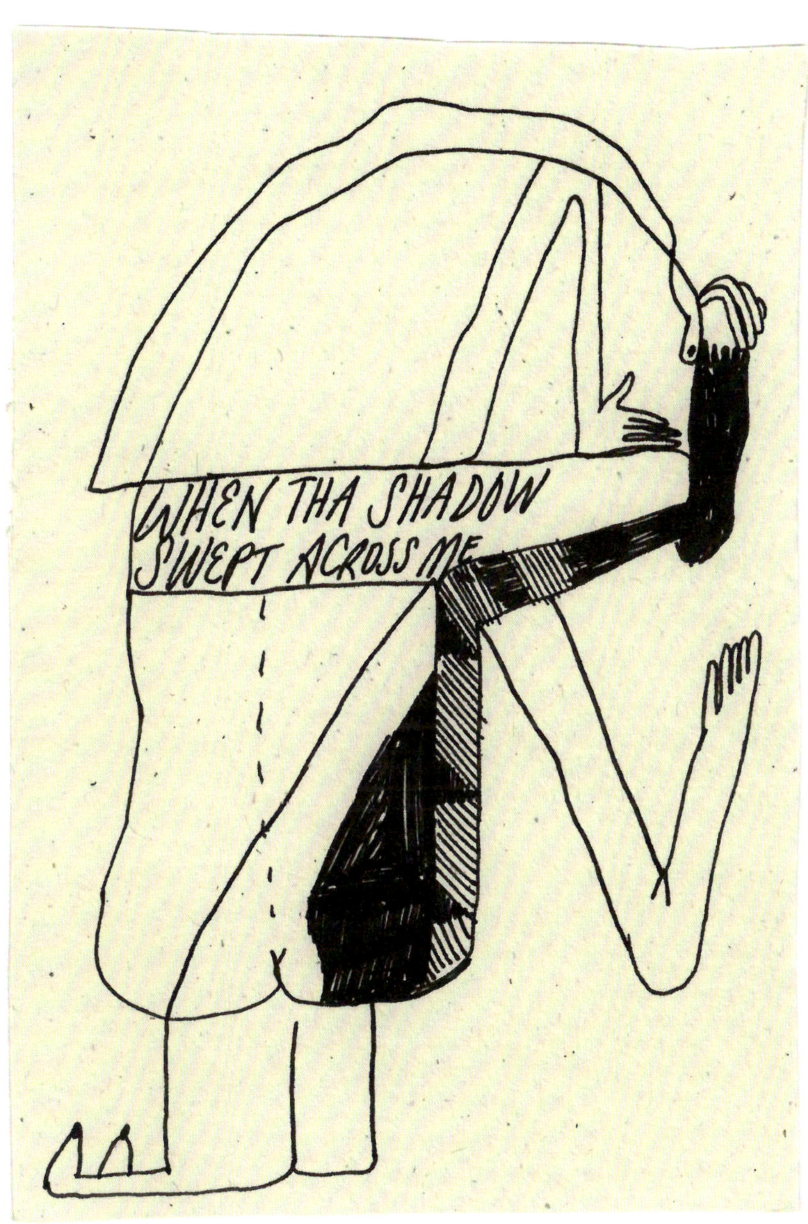

WHEN THA SHADOW SWEPT ACROSS ME

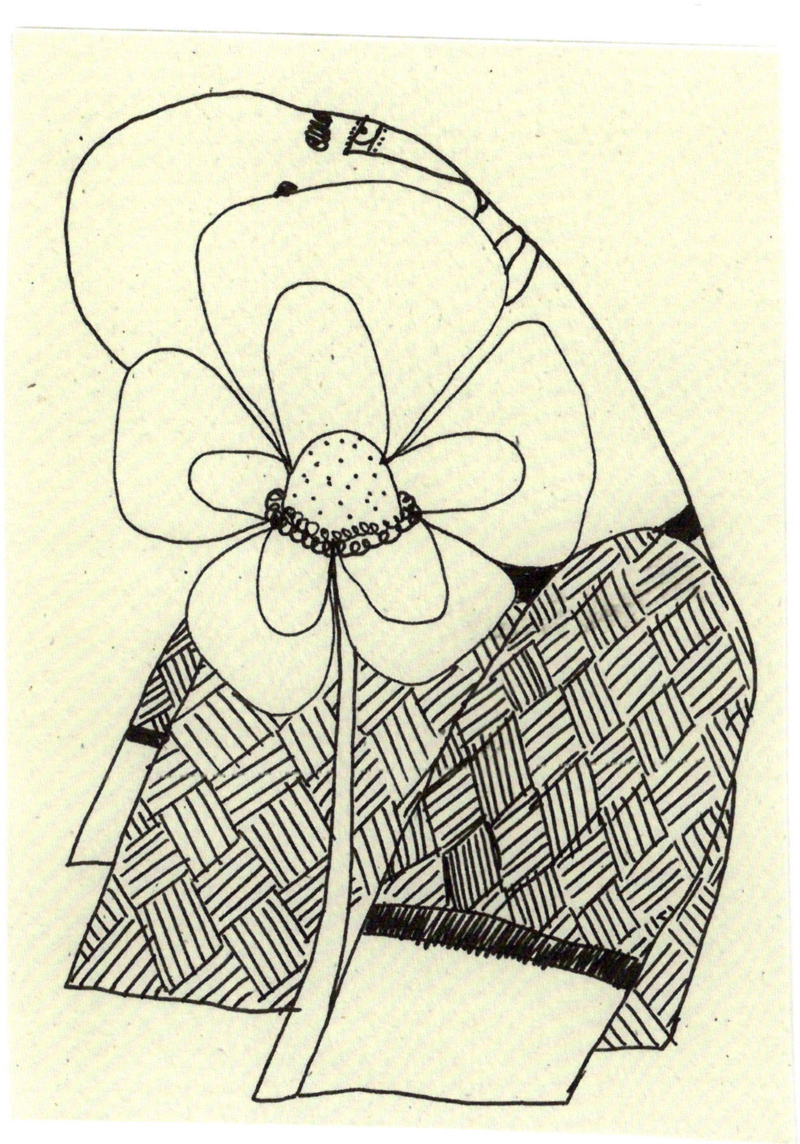

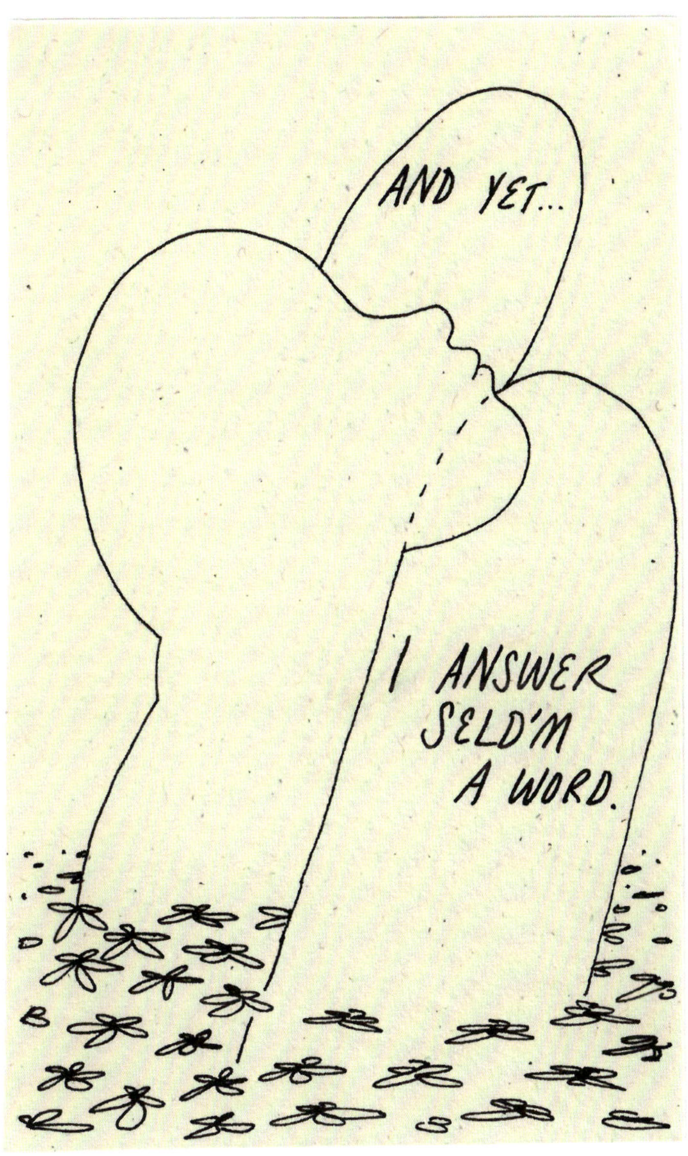
AND YET...
I ANSWER
SELD'M
A WORD.

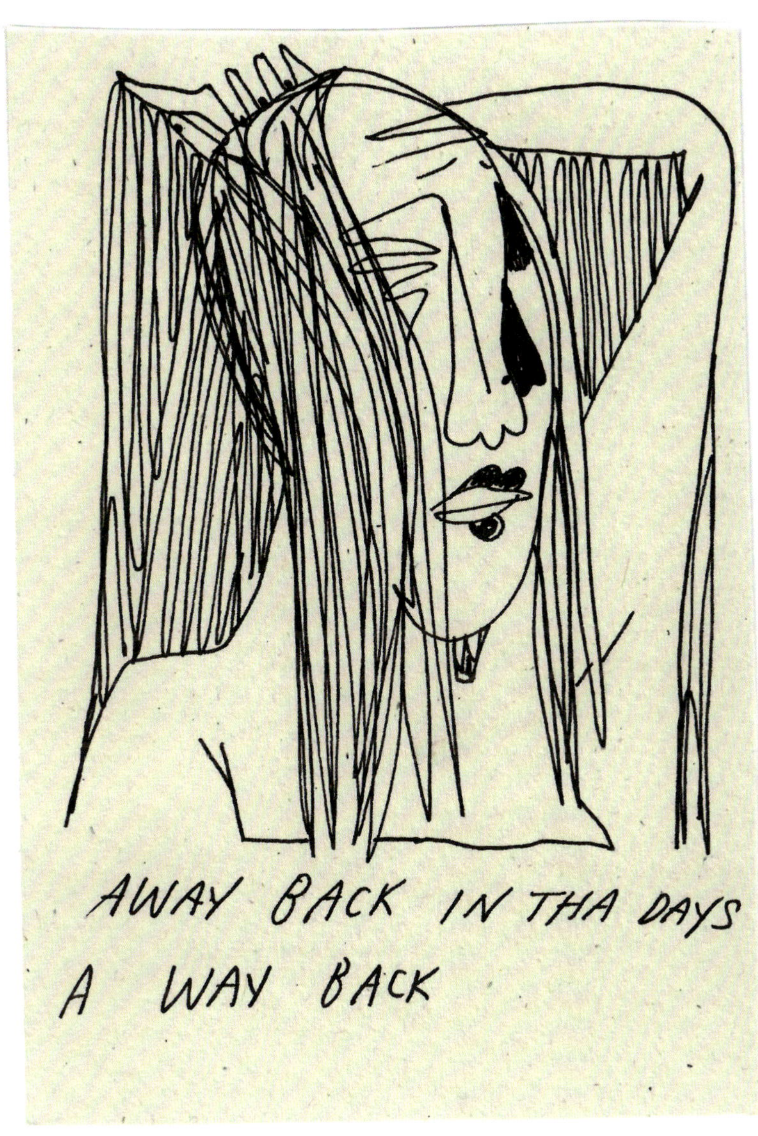

AWAY BACK IN THA DAYS
A WAY BACK

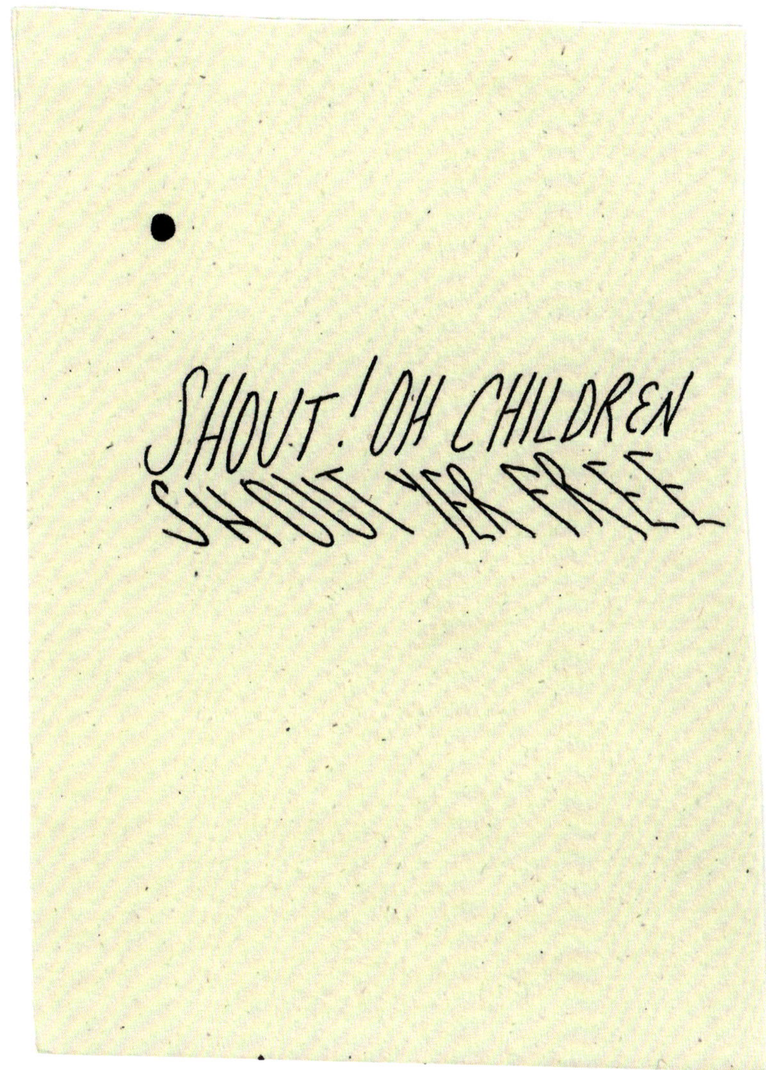

SHOUT! OH CHILDREN
SHOUT YER FREE

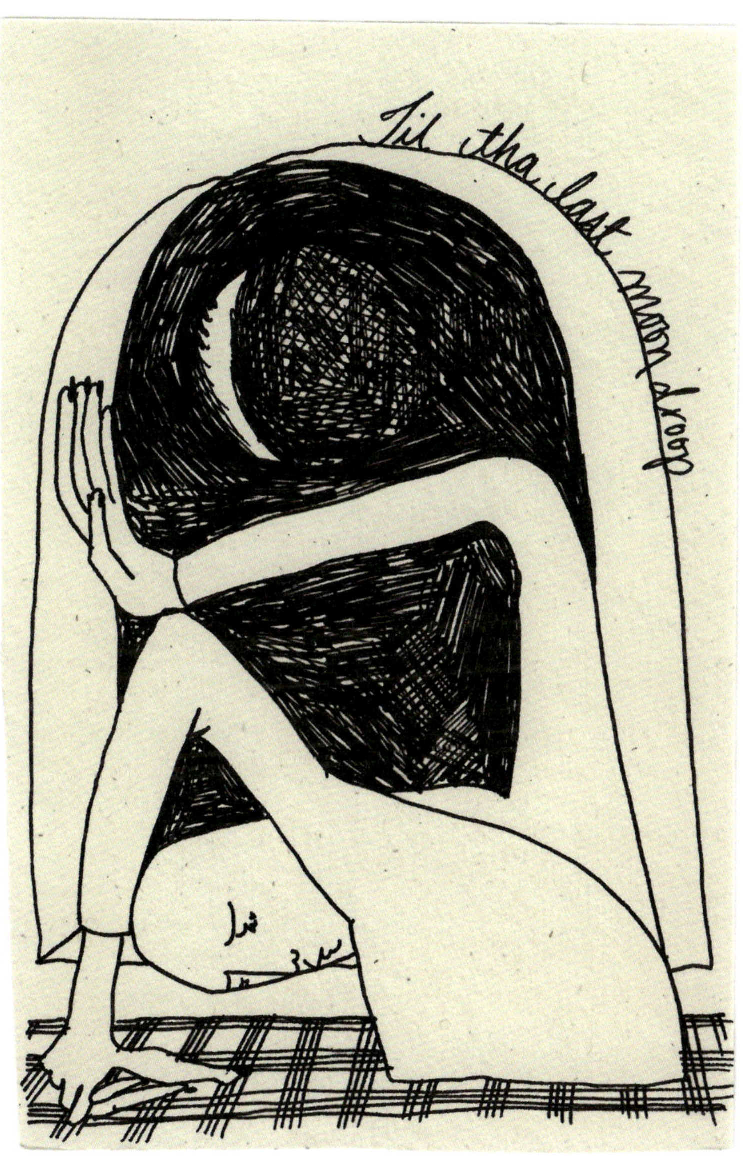
Til tha last moon droop

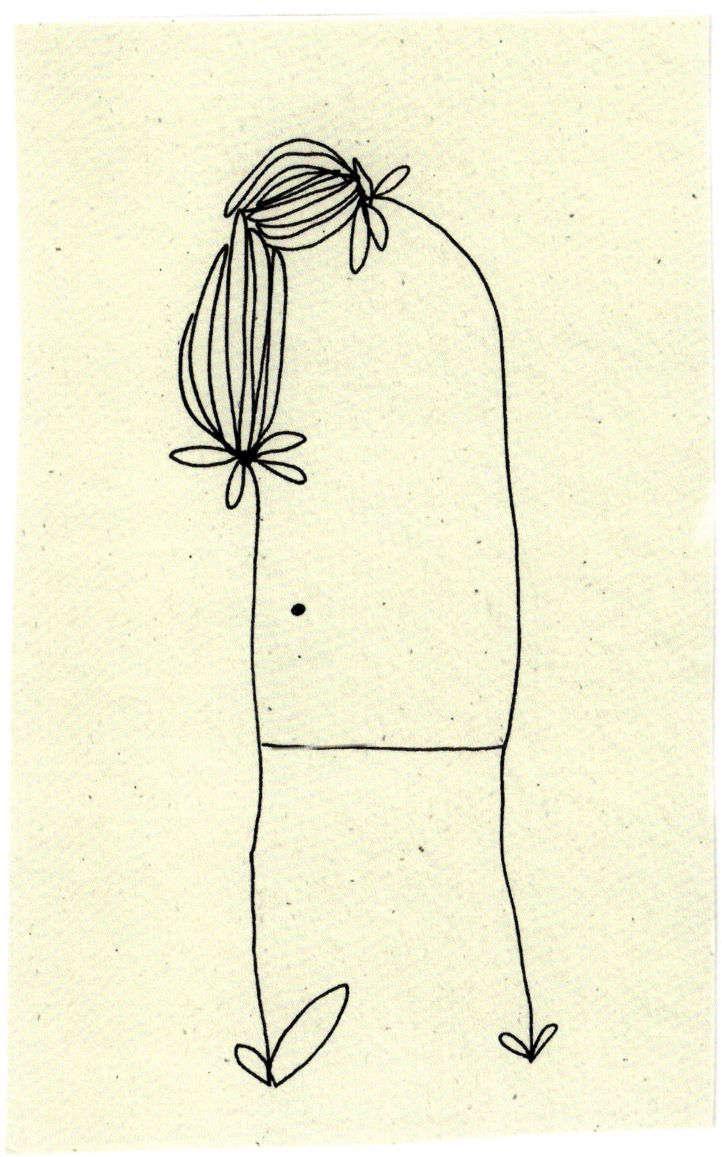

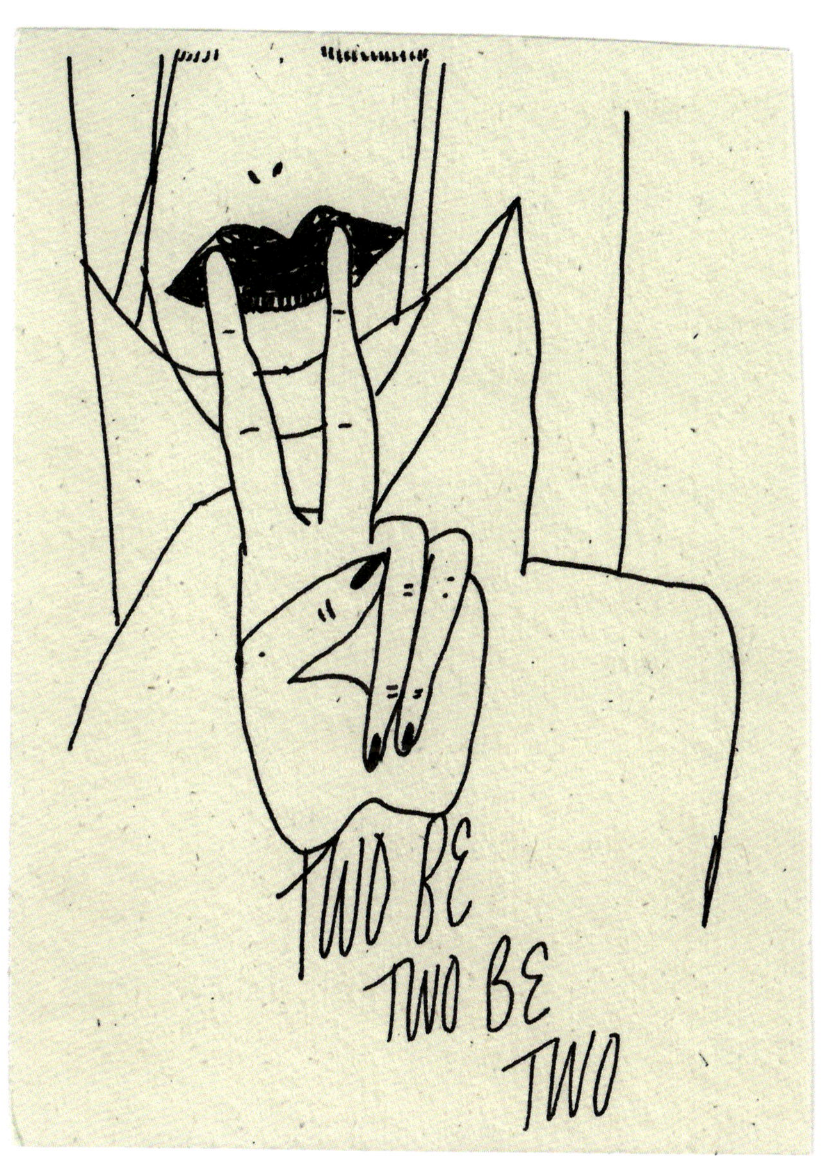

TWO BE
TWO BE
TWO

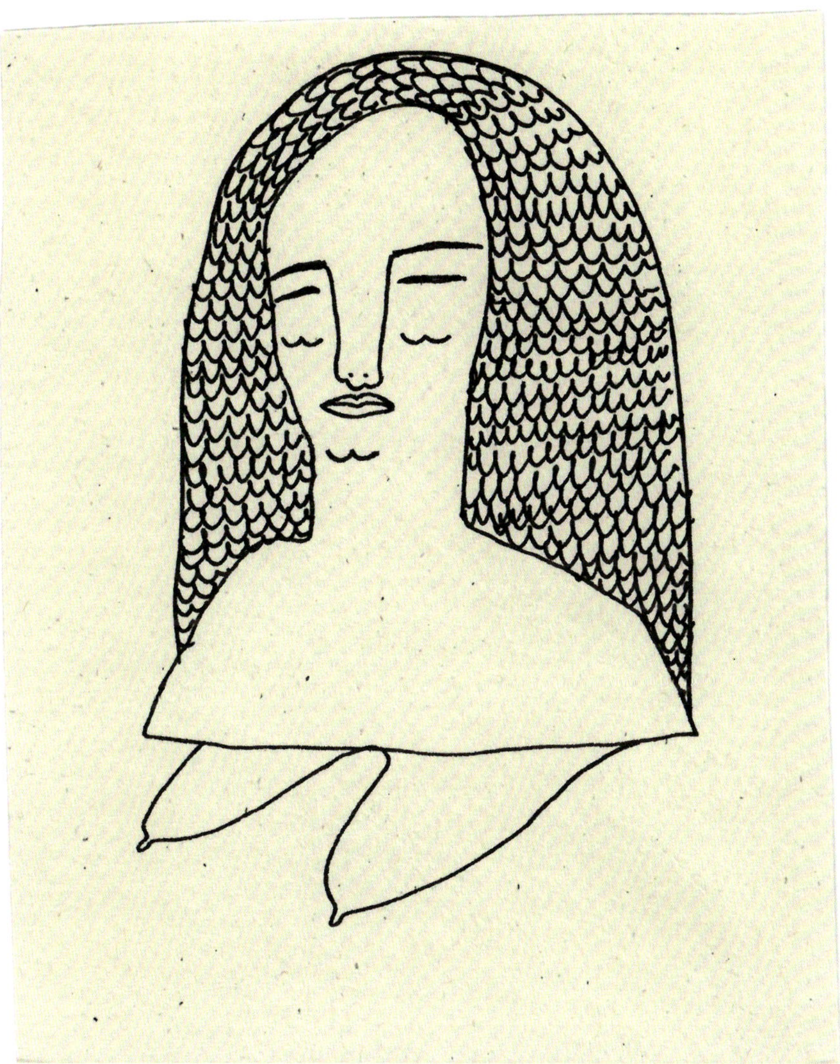

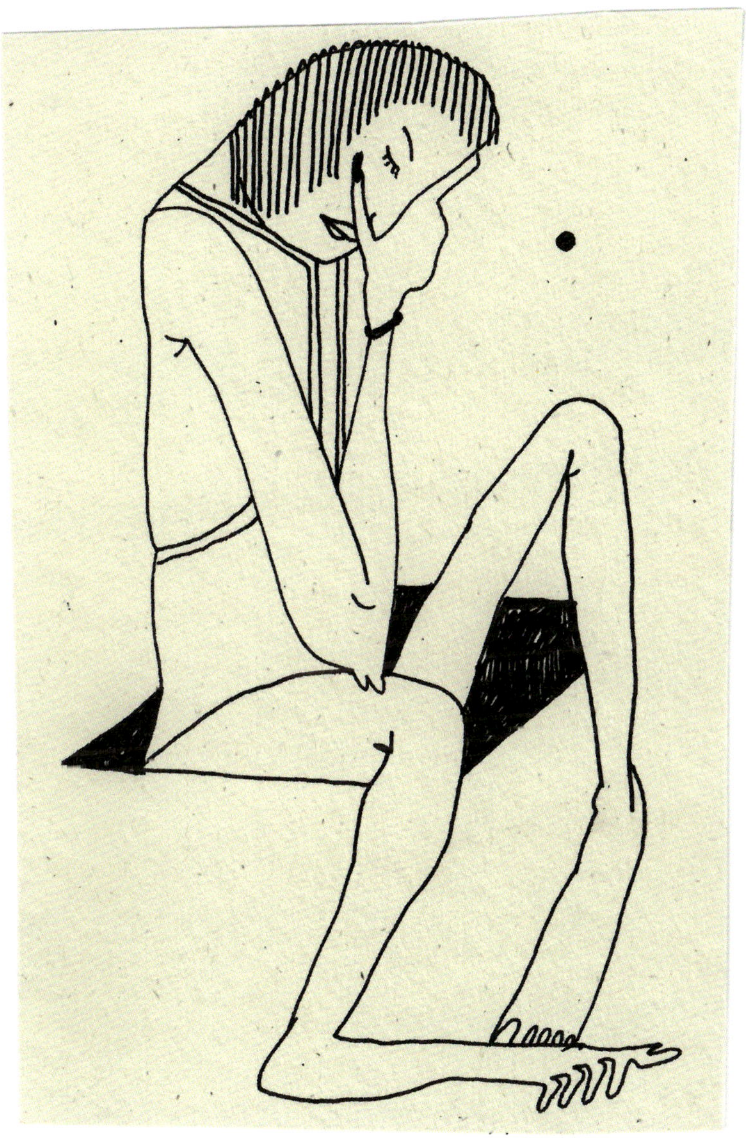

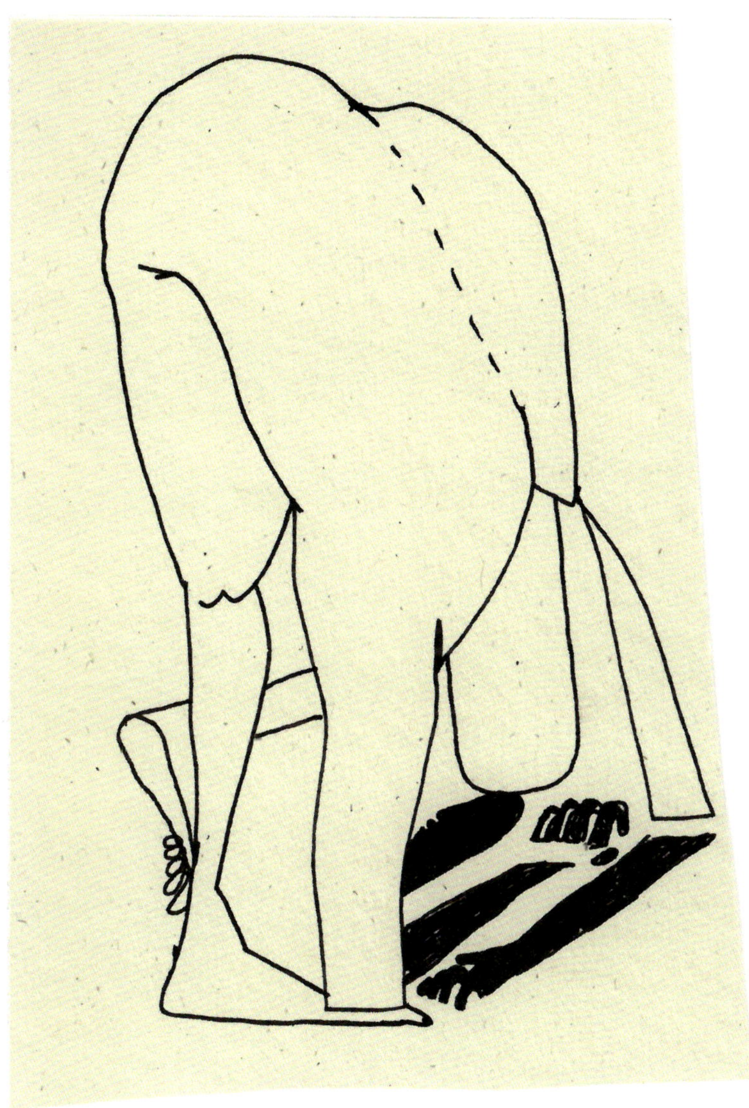

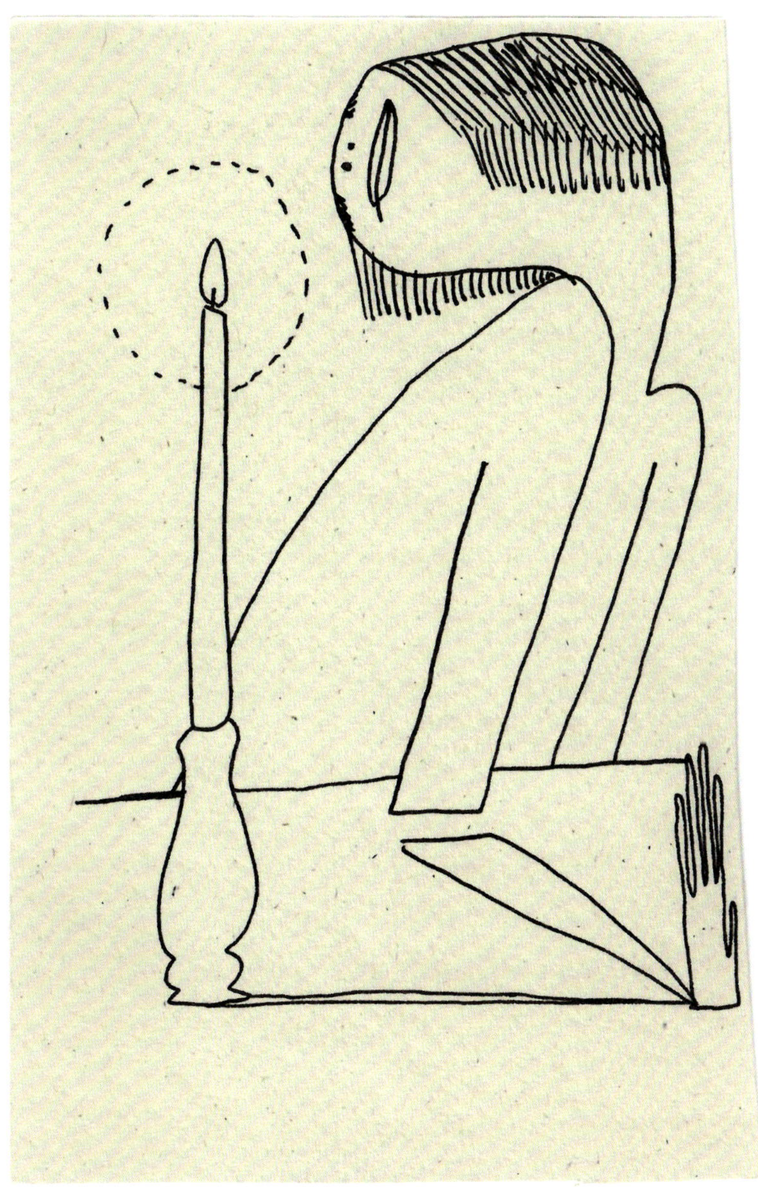

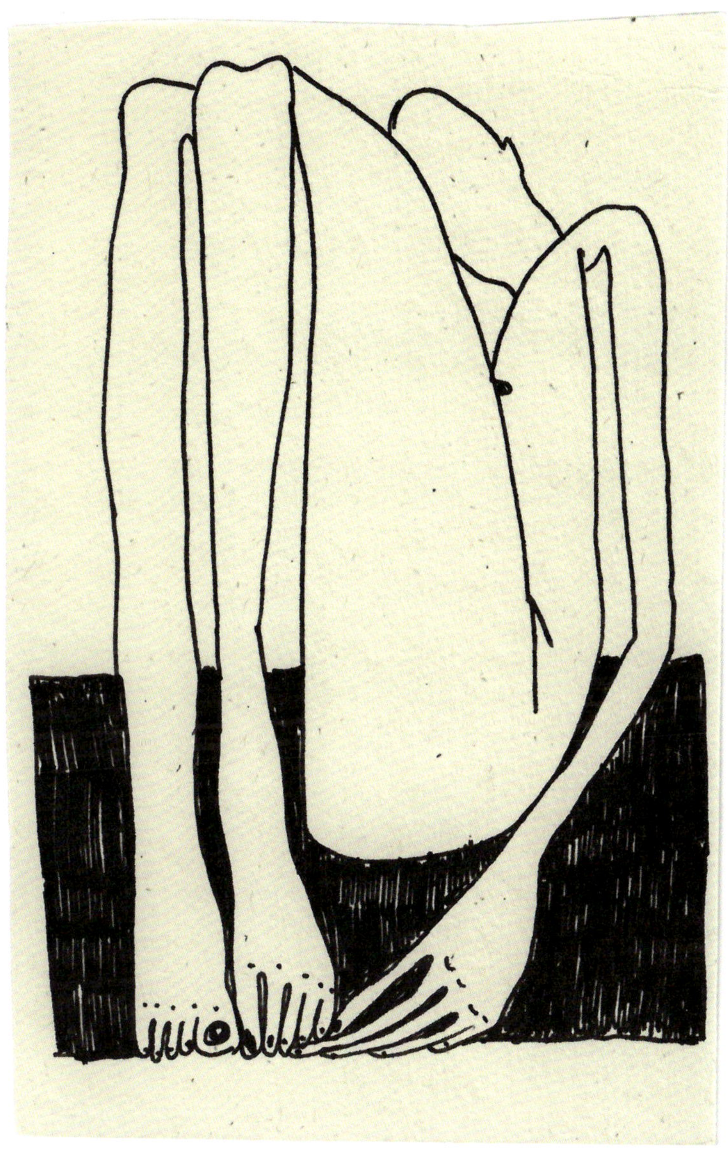

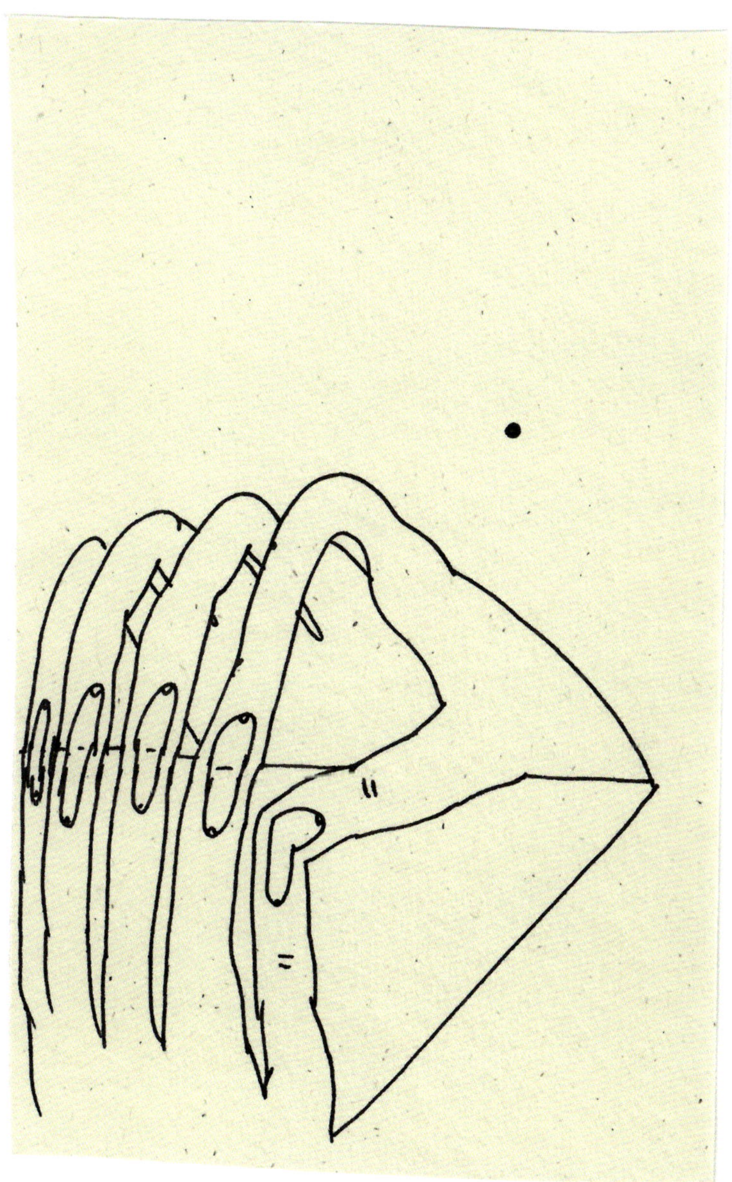

A COARSE IS A COARSE
(OH COURSE
OF COURSE,   OF COURSE)

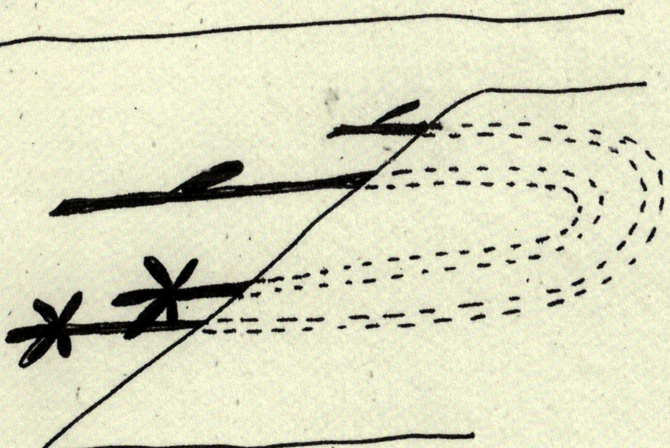

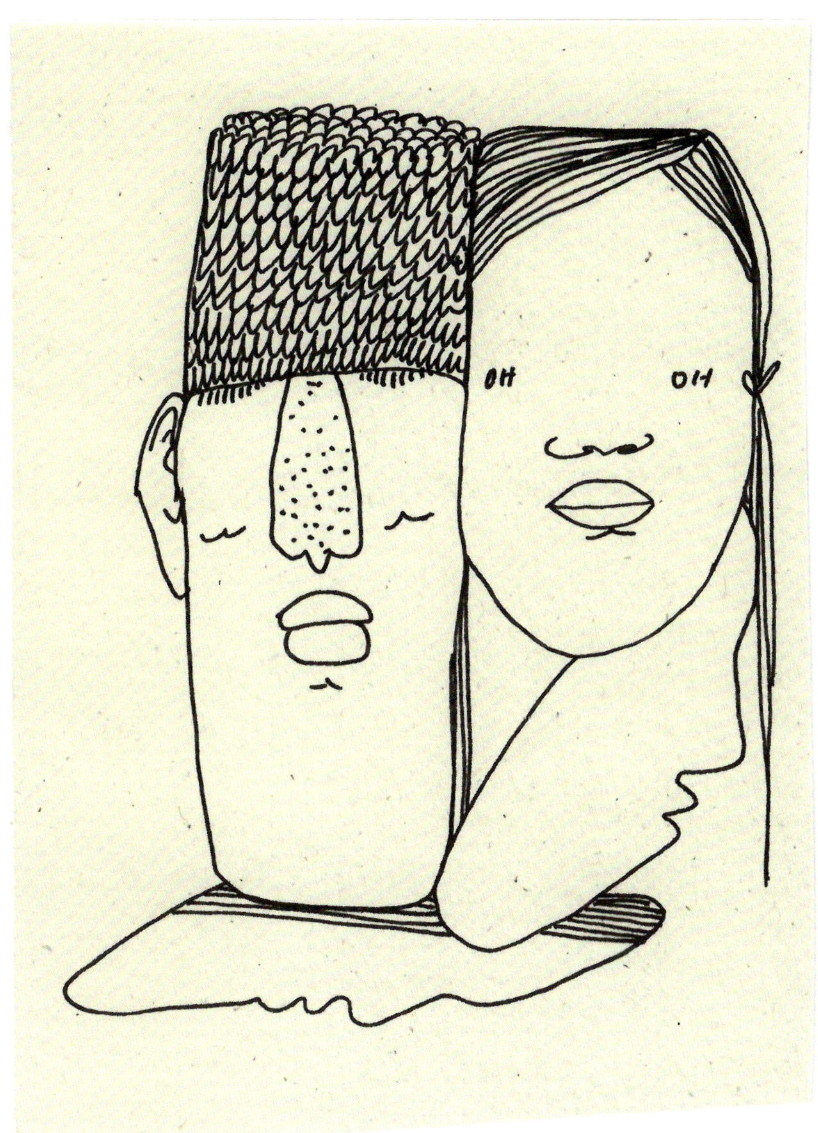
OH
OH

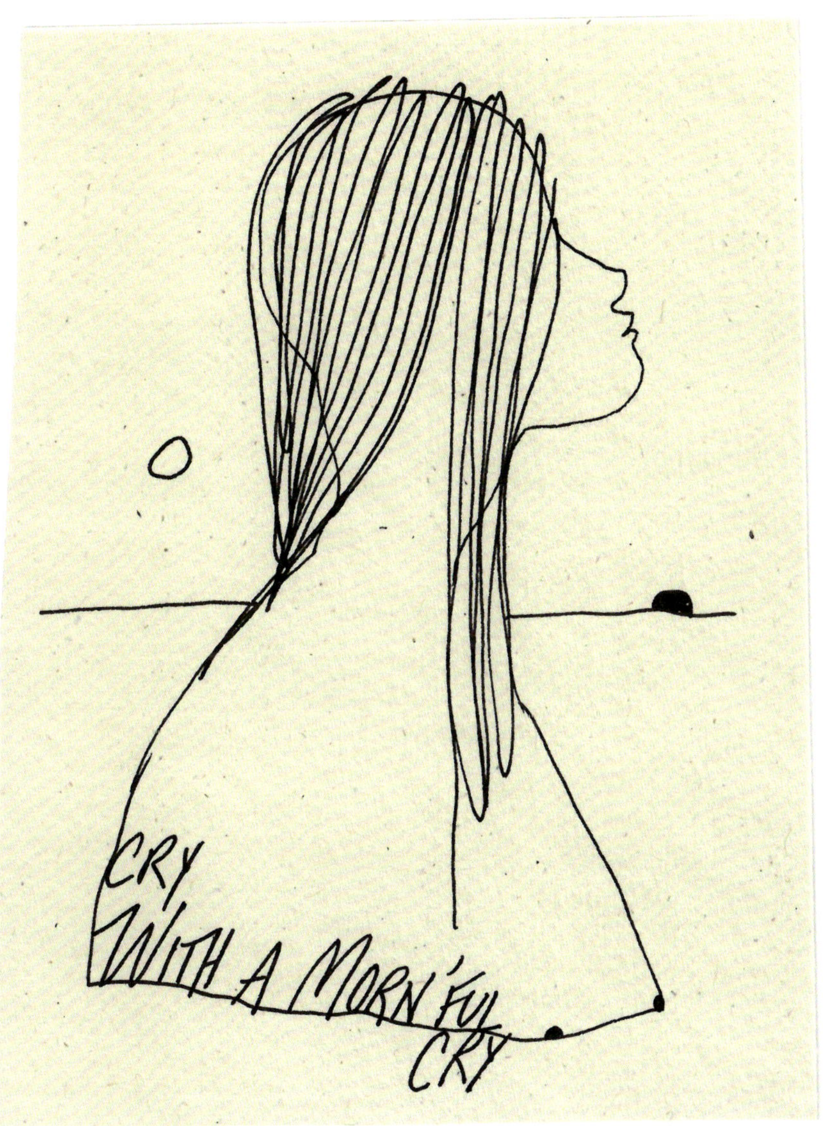

CRY
WITH A MORN'FUL
CRY

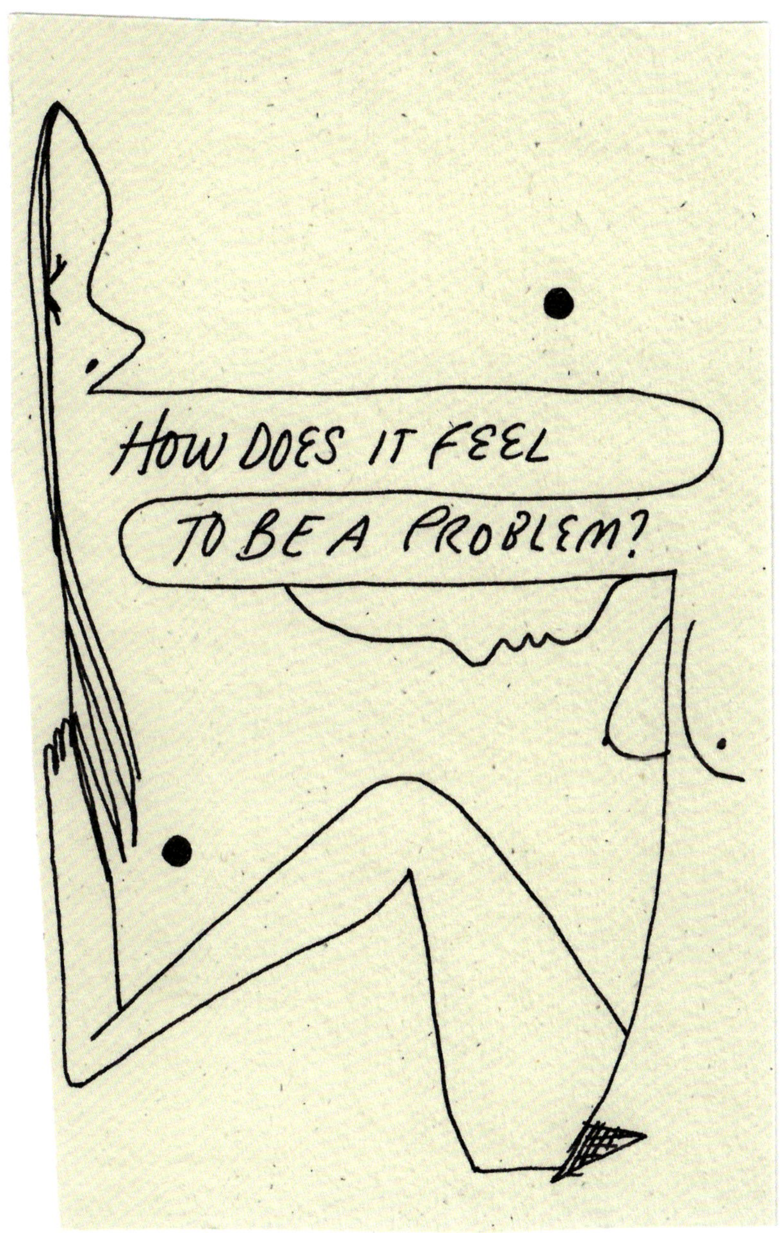

HOW DOES IT FEEL
TO BE A PROBLEM?

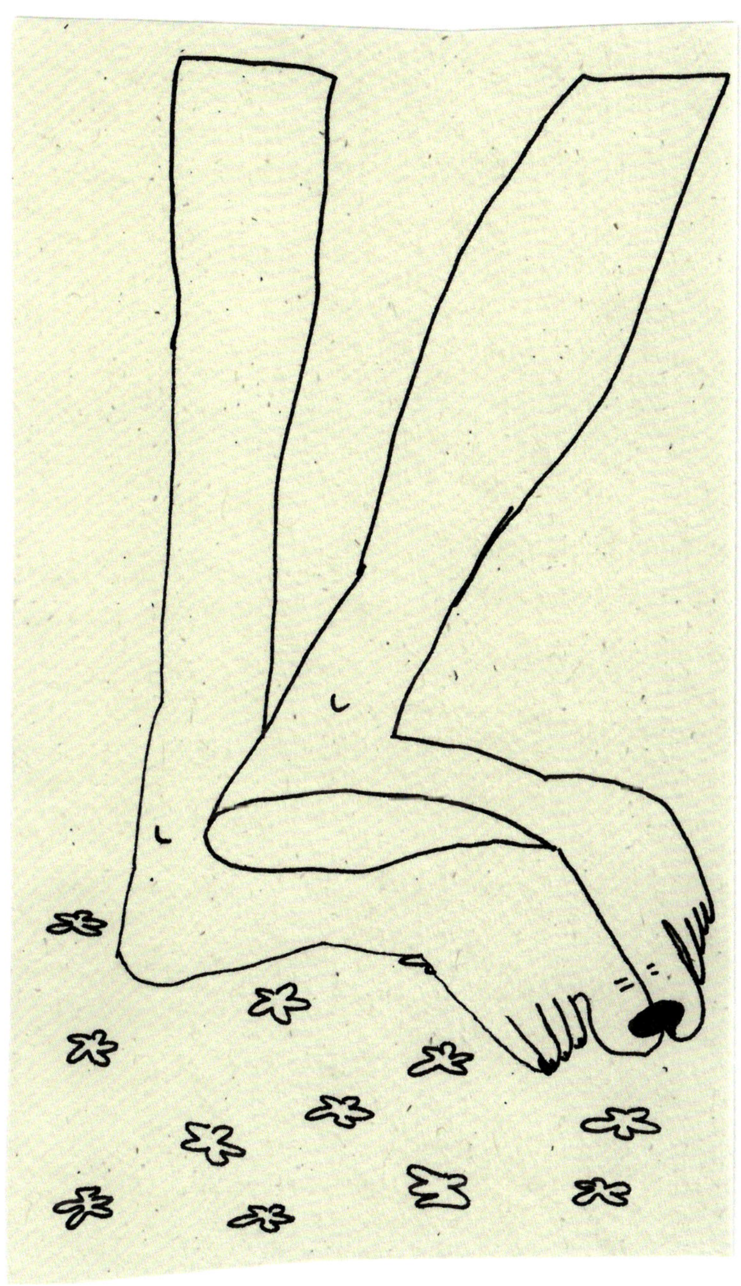

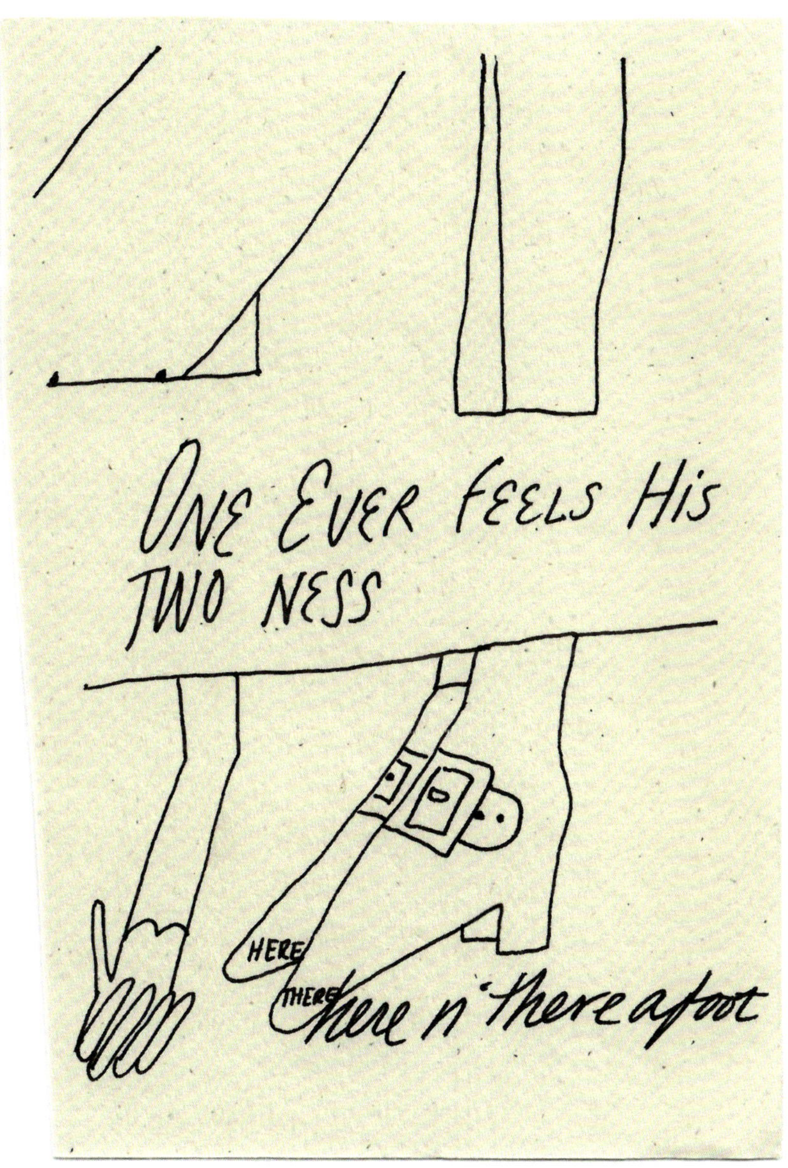

ONE EVER FEELS HIS
TWO NESS
HERE
THERE
here n' there afoot

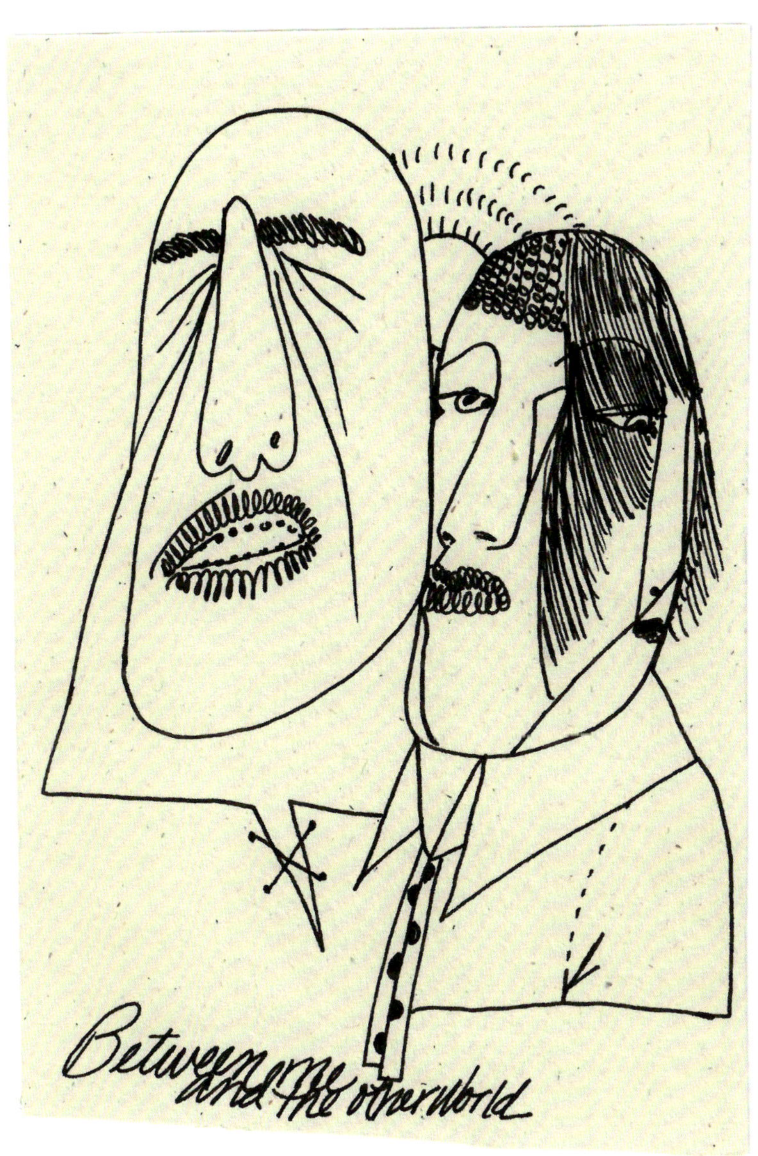
Between me
and the other world

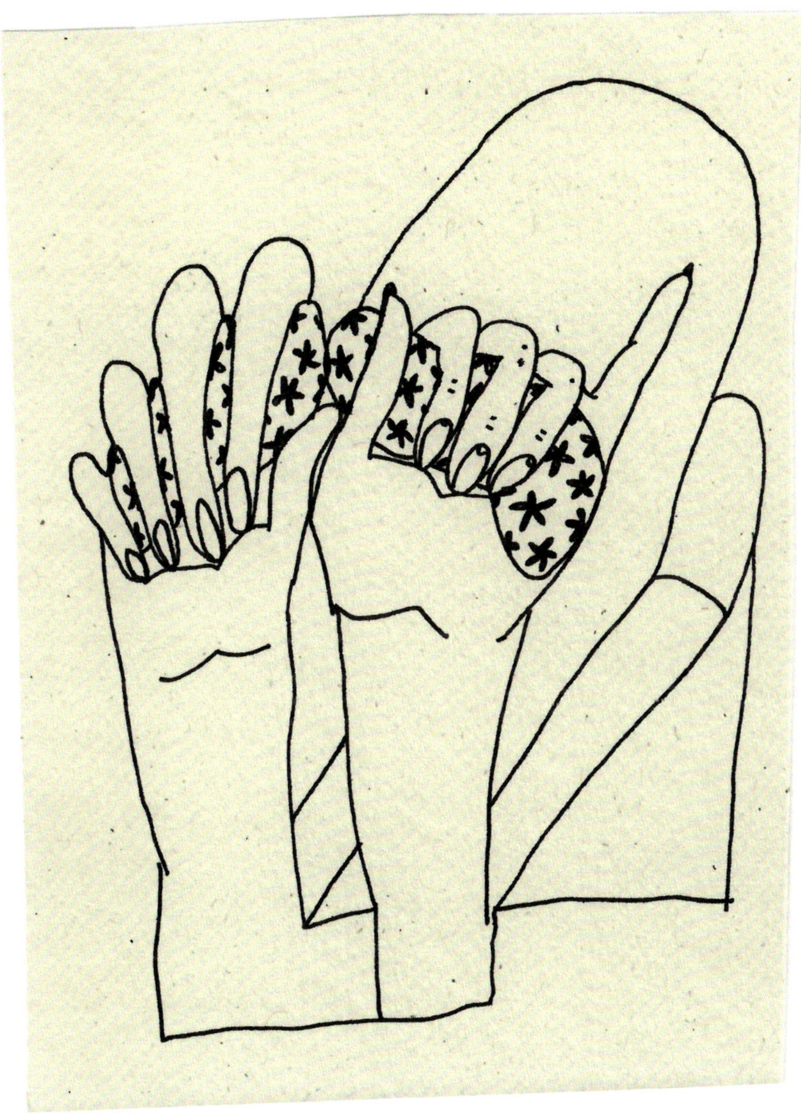

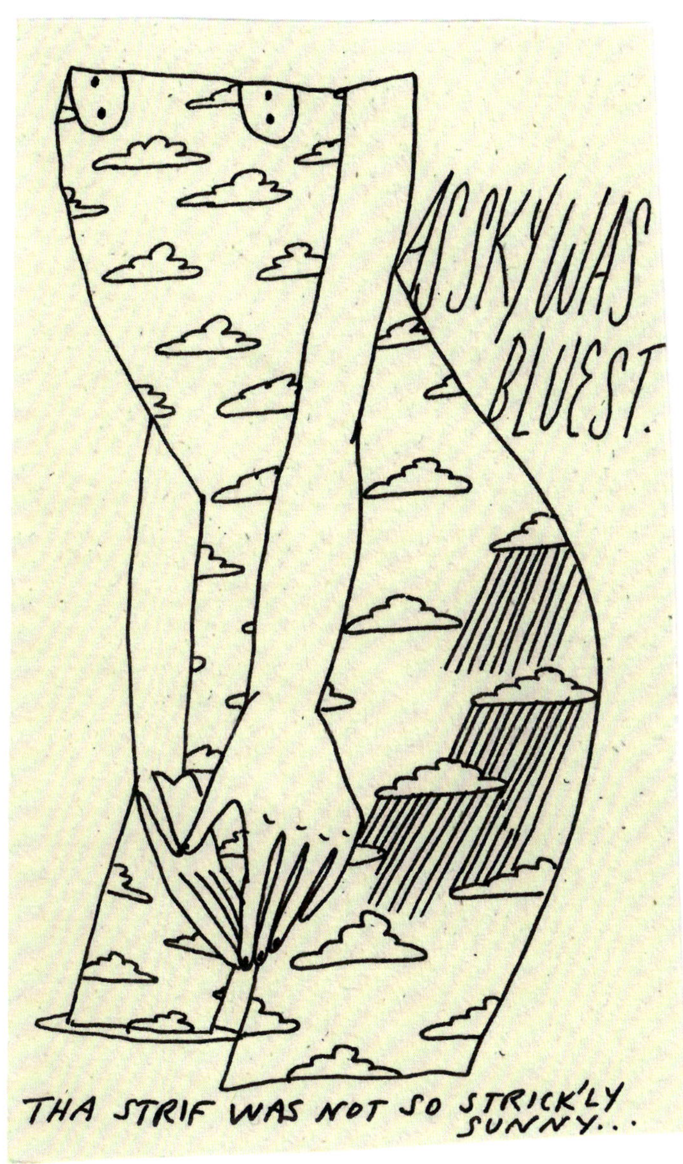
AS SKY WAS
BLUEST.
THA STRIF WAS NOT SO STRICK'LY
SUNNY...

W.E.B. DU BOIS

Born 1868 in Great Barrington, Massachusetts, USA, William
Edward Burghardt Du Bois was an American sociologist, historian,
author, editor and activist, thought of as the most important
Black protest leader in the United States during the first half of
the twentieth century. He shared in the creation of the National
Association for the Advancement of Colored People (NAACP)
in 1909 and edited *The Crisis*, its magazine, from 1910 to 1934.
His collection of essays *The Souls of Black Folk* (1903) is a
landmark of African American literature.

CHRISTINA QUARLES

Born 1985 in Chicago, Illinois, USA, Christina Quarles received
an MFA from the Yale School of Art in 2016, and holds a BA
from Hampshire College. Quarles was a 2016 participant at
the Skowhegan School for Painting and Sculpture. She was the
inaugural recipient of the 2019 Pérez Art Museum Miami Prize
and in 2017 she received the Rema Hort Mann Foundation
Emerging Artist Grant.

As a Queer, cis-woman born to a black father and a white mother,
Quarles engages with the world from a position that is multiply
situated. Her project is informed by her daily experience with
ambiguity, and seeks to dismantle assumptions of fixed subjectivity
through images that challenge the viewer to contend with the
disorganized body in a state of excess.

First published in 2021
by Afterall Books

Afterall
Central Saint Martins
University of the Arts London
Granary Building
1 Granary Square
London N1C 4AA
www.afterall.org

Afterall is a Research Centre of
University of the Arts London,
located at Central Saint Martins

Editors
Amber Husain
Mark Lewis

Project Coordinator
Camille Crichlow

Project Manager
Chloe Ting

Editorial Director
Mark Lewis

Associate Director
Charles Esche

Series Design
Pacific
Elizabeth Karp-Evans
Adam Turnbull
www.pacificpacific.pub

Printed and bound
die Keure, Belgium

ISBN 978-3-7533-0060-3

Germany, Austria, Switzerland /
Europe Buchhandlung Walther König
Ehrenstr. 4,
D - 50672 Köln
Fon +49 (0) 221 / 20 59 6 53
verlag@buchhandlung-walther-koenig.de

United States and Canada
D.A.P. / Distributed Art Publishers, Inc.
75 Broad Street, Suite 630
USA - New York, NY 10004
Fon +1 (0) 212 627 1999
orders@dapinc.com

Outside the United States and Canada,
Germany, Austria and Switzerland by
Thames & Hudson Ltd., London
www.thamesandhudson.com

Other titles in the series: